19.95

THE SILKEN CANOPY

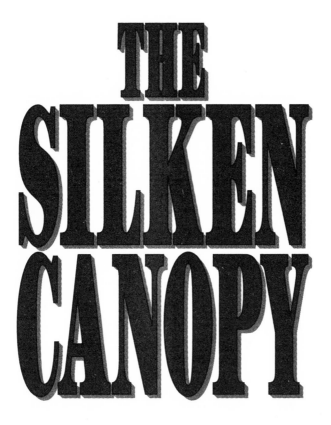

THE SILKEN CANOPY

A History of the Parachute

JOHN LUCAS

Airlife
England

First published in the UK 1973 under the title   .
The Big Umbrella by Elm Tree Books
Revised edition published in 1997
by Airlife Publishing Ltd

British Library Cataloguing-in-Publication Data
  A catalogue record for this book
  is available from the British Library

ISBN 1 85310 855 3

Typeset by Hewer Text Composition Services, Edinburgh
Printed and bound in England by Hartnolls Ltd,
Bodmin, Cornwall.

Airlife Publishing Ltd
101 Longden Road, Shrewsbury, SY3 9EB, England.

CONTENTS

FOREWORD

by Group Captain Douglas Bader CBE DSO DFC

I congratulate John Lucas on this splendid book. It is the first time in my recollection that anyone has attempted to write a history of the parachute from its early days. Indeed, I did not know that its history went back two hundred years, and I am quite sure no one else has realised this. I found this book fascinating and tremendously readable; it also contains much humour without which a book like this would not reach print.

Although the parachute itself did not come into existence until two hundred years ago, John Lucas has discovered some fascinating performances, even before the time of Leonardo da Vinci in the fifteenth century. I especially like the story of the Turk who announced that he would fly a furlong from the top of a high tower. His aeronautical device consisted of 'a long and large white garment, gathered into many plaits and folds made on purpose for gathering of the wind'. He had obviously done his sums incorrectly, because his attempt proved fatally unsuccessful.

In the last few months of World War I, the Germans sprang a great surprise on the Allied flyers by introducing a successful parachute, and saved many of their airmen's lives. Through the usual bureaucratic mishandling, delay and indecision, British flyers were not equipped with parachutes until some years after 1918. In World War II, the parachute saved countless lives.

I commend this book to the reader. It is an enjoyable combination of historical fact and amusing anecdote.

DB
London SW7
January 1973

ACKNOWLEDGEMENTS

To the many people who generously gave of their time and expertise during my researches for this book, my warm gratitude. I appreciate especially the invaluable help of Charles Gibbs-Smith, the aeronautical historian, for reading the early chapters of my manuscript. My thanks, too, to A. W. Nayler, librarian of the Royal Aeronautical Society, and his assistant, Mrs E. Dane, for their interest, suggestions and loans of material, and to Dr Christopher Dowling and his colleagues at the Imperial War Museum.

I am also indebted to the following: Mrs Velda Irvin, of Los Angeles – whose late husband, Leslie L. Irvin, made the first modern freefall jump and founded the company which bears his name – for checking and enlarging upon details of her husband's life; Leslie Pargeter, late of the Royal Flying Corps, for his personal reminiscences on flying without parachutes in World War I; Mrs Renée Hampshire, for background material concerning her father, Major T. Orde-Lees, who strove to obtain parachutes for Leslie Pargeter and his ill-fated comrades-in-arms; Wing Cdr J. Jewell, of Martin-Baker Ltd, for his guidance on the development of the British ejection seat; Air Vice-Marshal Donald Bennett, former leader of the RAF's Pathfinder Force, who kindly described for me the parachute's role in air operations over Germany; my friend Eric Stevens, for personal recollections as a paramedic in World War II; Sqn Ldr W. Paul, Secretary General, British Parachute Association; John Meacock, former British parachute jumping champion; Sqn Ldr Ronald Smith, of No. 1 Parachute Training School, RAF Abingdon; Miss Joan Walthew, whose scrapbooks and other material relating to parachutes in World War II proved most valuable; John Simpson, managing director, and staff of Irvin Great Britain Ltd, particularly Mr Gordon Eastley and their public relations adviser, Shirley Koster; members of the staff of RFD-GQ Ltd, in particular Arthur C. Dickinson, formerly joint managing director; Northrop-Ventura Ltd, USA; the US Dept of Agriculture;

the National Aeronautics and Space Administration, Washington DC; Malcolm Lumb, of Cable & Wireless; British Meteorological Office; the British Museum; the Newspaper Library (Colindale); the National Library of Science and Invention; and the Patent Office Library, for their usual unstinting help.

JL (1973)

Acknowledgements (revised edition)

The author wishes to thank the following for their kindness in supplying guidance, help and information: Arnold Nayler (once again) and Brian Riddle, Royal Aeronautical Society; Brian Miller and Del Holyland of Martin-Baker Aircraft Ltd.; Ray Blackman and Sqn Ldr Graham Hand, of GQ Parachutes Ltd; Ian B. Wright, retired director of Irvin Aerospace Ltd and honorary curator of the Irvin archives and museum, and Mrs Judy Adams; Wayne Williams, US Forest Service; Air Vice-Marshal G.W. Carleton, Director, RAF Legal Services; Air Vice-Marshal A. G. Dudgeon (RAF ret'd); Major Bob Card, Commandant, Joint Service Parachute Centre, Netheravon; Sqn Ldrs Roland Wadley and George Sizeland, former parachuting jumping instructors at No. 1 Parachute Training School, Brize Norton; Dr John Zarnecki, Physical Laboratory, University of Kent, who is associated with the Cassini/Huygens space mission to Titan; John Hitchen and Tony Butler, British Parachute Association; Jackie (Smith) Young, former world parachute champion; John Meacock, Peterborough Parachute Centre, Sibson (Cambs); Arthur Bentley and Barry Clark, chief instructors, parascending, British Hang-gliding and Paragliding Association; Rodger Tamblyn, skydiver and photographer; my cousin, Major Herbert Lucas, US Air Force (ret'd), of California; my brother Raymond Lucas; and my friend Mark Sennett.

Transcripts of Crown copyright records in the Public Record Office appear by permission of the Controller of HM Stationery Office; the extract from *Years of Command,* by Lord Douglas of Kirtleside and R. C. Wright, appears by permission of A. D. Peters & Co., and the extract from *The German Air Force in the Great War,* by G. P. Neumann, is reproduced by permission of Times Newspapers Ltd.

For permission to reproduce the photographs in this book, the author wishes to thank: Irvin Aerospace Ltd, the US Forest Service, *Daily Mirror, Daily Telegraph,* NASA (Washington), the Red

ACKNOWLEDGEMENTS

Devils, the National Library of Science and Invention (London), GQ Parachutes Ltd, Imperial War Museum, Royal Aeronautical Society, T. W. Willans, Martin-Baker Aircraft Ltd, Mrs Renée Hampshire and Simon Ward.

Finally, my special thanks to Molly Sedgwick, joint author with Peter Hearn and Dolly Shepherd, of *When the 'Chute Went Up* (revised edition, Skyline 1996) for guidance on the life of her mother, and for permission to use quoted material.

CHAPTER ONE

YESTERDAY'S DREAMS

For most of the past 200 years, since André-Jacques Garnerin first leapt with a parachute from beneath a balloon over Paris in 1797, that simple inverted bag of air held by a gathering of cords served as a plaything. But with the advent of flight, its billowing white canopy came to represent a guardian angel, and has saved thousands of lives – 200,000, according to the aeronautical historian the late Charles Gibbs-Smith – and succoured countless people with food and medical supplies which floated down to them in peace and war. For them the sight of a parachute was as welcome as manna from heaven. Indeed, the parachute has even been to the heavens and back, for when scientists cast around for other worlds to explore, it was there, as always, to usher man safely down again.

According to Greek mythology, the ingenious inventor Daedalus made wings for himself and his son Icarus so that they could escape from the labyrinth in Crete where they were held captive by King Minos. Icarus foolishly ignored his father's warning not to fly too near the sun; as a result, the wax which attached his wings to his body melted and he fell to his death. But although Icarus bridged the gap between earth and the heavens, the myth did not endow him with a parachute to ensure his return. It was man who was to devise a means of escape from the hazards of the air; the parachute's place was in the real world, not mythology.

There is hardly a simpler device than the parachute, yet lifetimes have been devoted to its refinement into a precision instrument, and lives sacrificed in the testing of various early prototypes. For decades it was a toy of showman balloonists, idling in the wings of time like an actor waiting for his cue. Yet even though it preceded the Wright brothers' achievement of powered flight with a heavier-than-air machine, aviation, or rather its bureaucratic superstructure, was fatally slow to realise its lifesaving qualities.

So distant in time are its origins that the parachute's story

13

hardly has a recognisable beginning; nor, in the space age, is it over. The parasol, which was in use 2,800 years ago, is thought to have inspired the parachute, no doubt because of the resistance it offered to a brisk wind. It is described in the famous *Annals* of the Chinese historian Ssu-ma Ch'ien, which dates back to 90 BC and refers to a story about the legendary emperor Shun. The emperor's father wanted to kill him, and set fire to a granary tower in which Shun was hiding. Apparently the emperor escaped by improvising a parachute out of a number of large cone-shaped straw hats and jumping to the ground with it. So the Chinese, leaders in technology in the East, were not, it seems, unfamiliar with the principle of the parachute.

Tragedy and the parachute's story are interwoven. One of the first of many disasters occurred in Constantinople in 1147, or so we understand from Knolles's *General History of the Turks*. Emanuel, the Greek emperor, was being visited by the Turkish Sultan Clisasthan, one of whose retinue had spread the word that at a given time and place – the tilt yard – he would fly a furlong from the top of a high tower. He had no parachute, but 'a long and large white garment, gathered into many plaits and folds, made on purpose for gathering of the wind'. It was not enough: despite the emperor's entreaties not to tempt Providence, the Turk leapt off the tower and broke every bone in his body. And in his book *A New Historical Relation of the Kingdom of Siam*, Simon de la Loubère, French ambassador in Siam in the 1680s, talks of the doings of Chinese and Siamese acrobats: 'There dyed one, some Years since,' he wrote, 'who leap'd from the Hoop supporting himself only two Umbrellas, the hands of which were firmly fix'd to his girdle; the Wind carr'd him accidentally sometimes to the Ground, sometimes on Trees or Houses, and sometimes into the River. He so exceedingly diverted the King of Siam that this Prince had made him a great Lord: he had lodged him in the Palace and had given him a great Title; or, as they say, a great Name.' There had been a reference to this method of escape in 1214, when Yo Kho, grandson of a great general, Yo Fei, talked of what he saw in Canton as a young man when his father was governor in 1192. Yo Kho said he was told of a thief who stole one leg off a golden cockerel surmounting a minaret. When asked how he escaped he said he descended by holding on to two umbrellas without handles. 'After I jumped into the air the high wind kept them fully open, making them like wings for me, and so I reached the ground without injury.'

In the West, the earliest parachutes were a pyramid-shaped type sketched by Leonardo da Vinci, and a conical one drawn by an unknown artist whose work is preserved in the British Museum, both dating from the 1480s. They are thought to have derived from an earlier and common source not yet discovered. The conical parachute of the anonymous artist shows a figure holding on to a wooden crosspiece spanning its mouth. A second drawing, of a totally unconvincing fall-breaker, depicts a similar figure clutching two long ribbon-like strips of cloth which flutter above his head. Leonardo's pyramid-shaped parachute was sketched in 1485 and appears in the *Codex Atlanticus*. A translation of his description reads: 'If a man has a tent roof of caulked linen twelve *braccia* broad and twelve *braccia* high, he will be able to let himself fall from any great height without danger to himself.' A *braccio* approximated to an arm's length, so Leonardo's device would have measured between 23ft and 28ft (7m and 9m) wide at the base and as much high. The canopy would have stretched over a wooden framework, with a pole from the apex from which the jumper would have hung, clutching a cord from each corner. Whether Leonardo made an experimental model is not known. His inventions were more likely the stuff of dreams. But given these dimensions and the use of light wood, a life-size version would almost certainly have provided enough drag through the air to bring a man down safely. Many modern man-carrying parachutes have similar dimensions.

But Leonardo cannot be called the true originator of the parachute because it was centuries before his drawings and other writings re-emerged from obscurity. When he died, near Amboise in France in 1519, he left all his manuscripts in the supposedly safe keeping of his friend Francesco da Melzi. Either through ignorance or carelessness, Francesco stored them away for half a century, on his own death leaving them to his son, who cared nothing at all for their importance, even supposing he recognised it. Despite this monumental offhandedness, most of Leonardo's precious drawings and notes have been preserved, though some did fall into other hands. Not until towards the end of the nineteenth century was a selection of his aeronautical sketches published, including his design for a parachute, and then only for limited circulation among academics. However, about a century earlier, in 1784, the Frenchman Jean-Pierre Blanchard had used the parachute in experiments for dropping animals, which proves beyond doubt that Leonardo's own paper dreams for the parachute were, historically, redundant.

After Leonardo, no developments took place until 1595 when a

Hungarian mathematician, Fausto Veranzio of Venice, published a book called *Machinae Novae* which contained an engraving of 'Homo volans' ('flying man') who appeared to be jumping from a tower, suspended from a square sheet on a stiff frame with a cord from each corner. Veranzio's suggestion that the size of the frame should be varied according to the weight of the 'cargo' showed an early grasp of sound principles, for in general the bigger the canopy the greater the drag and the greater the weight that can be sustained. It seems doubtful whether Veranzio had ever seen Leonardo's sketch, for although his idea is reminiscent of Leonardo's, the execution is quite different. Leonardo drew a pyramid, Veranzio a sail-like sheet. Veranzio's sail theme was taken up subsequently several times. For example, Des Maretz's *Ariane* (1639) contains an illustration of a prisoner escaping from a fortress by jumping and clutching the corners of a bed-sheet.

The first use of a parachute in an air machine was by Canon Desforges, of Étampes, in 1772. This ambitious but ill-named contraption, the 'voiture volant', was made of wicker-work and had wings worked by hand. Above the wicker-work hung a giant cloth canopy which, it was hoped, would help to keep it airborne. Desforges was in fact slightly injured when he tried it out from a tower. Nine years later, Blanchard made his 'flying ship', which was to be steered by a rudder motivated by movements of the body, and incorporating a parachute. Unfortunately, it never took to the air.

The invention of a parachute capable of landing a living being safely was taken a stage further in 1782 and 1783 with the invention of the hot air balloon by two French brothers, Étienne and Joseph Montgolfier. Shortly before this, however, one of them, Joseph, an experimenter in other branches of aeronautics besides balloons, had investigated the principle of air resistance – which a parachute, of course, employs – and he is reported to have descended safely with one from a housetop near Lyons, and dropped a sheep wearing a parachute from a tower at Avignon in 1779. Being paper manufacturers by trade, the Montgolfiers had abundant material at their disposal for their successful 'fire balloon' experiments. They began by inflating small paper bags, and then a large silk bag, with hot air produced by burning chopped straw and wool. At first, they failed to understand what it was that made the balloon rise; they were convinced that it was due to 'gas' given off by the straw and wool burning beneath it rather than the warm air becoming lighter than the cold air outside. They made two experimental balloons, one of which rose to about 600ft (183m). The second, made of paper-lined linen, ascended to 1,000ft (305m) on 25 April 1783, and came down three quarters of a mile away. On 5 June the brothers gave a public demonstration with a larger balloon, 110ft (33.5m) in circumference, which was so buoyant that eight men were needed to hold it down. Thousands of people from the surrounding countryside poured into Annonay to watch the ascent.

In the meantime, three others – Dr Jacques Charles, a physicist, and the two brothers Robert, who were instrument makers – had perfected a way of making balloons using hydrogen rather than hot air. They had constructed a balloon from rubberised fabric and filled it with hydrogen produced by pouring sulphuric acid on to iron filings. On 26 August, the balloon rose 100ft (30.5m) into the air, and the next day there was a public display at the Champ de Mars on the site of what is now the Eiffel Tower. The balloon ascended to a height of 3,000ft (915m) and came down fifteen miles away at Gonesse only to be torn to ribbons by frightened villagers.

On 19 September, before a crowd which included King Louis XVI and Queen Marie Antoinette, as well as courtiers, the Montgolfier brothers released their beautifully ornamented balloon, painted in oils, with a first ever cargo of live balloonists – a sheep, a cock and a duck – from Versailles. Two months later, on 21 November, in an enlarged version of the Montgolfiers' Versailles balloon, and fitted with a circular gallery, two volunteers, François Pilâtre de Rozier and the Marquis d'Arlandes, became the world's first true balloonists when they made a non-tethered ascent from the Bois de Boulogne. It was a particularly hazardous trip, as they were feverishly feeding burning straw and wool into the large and greedy burner in order to maintain height, while mopping the edges of the balloon with water to prevent charring. At least, de Rozier was. He complained of lack of help from the Marquis who, being less practical, seemed more interested in admiring the view. They landed five miles away from a reported height of 3,000ft (915m), about twenty-five minutes after take-off, to a well-earned and enthusiastic reception.

This was a busy year for would-be balloonists and jumpers. Sebastien Lenormand, a watchmaker from Montpellier, France, experimented by dropping animals on his 14ft (4.25m) diameter cone-shaped parachute of linen or oiled silk. It is Lenormand, first user of the Greek/French word 'parachute' (literally, 'against fall'), who is credited with the first authentic human jump – but from a tower in Montpellier, not from a balloon. Lenormand is also reported to have demonstrated from the windows of a house that a parachute could be used to escape from fire. The next year, 1784, an English balloonist, Thomas Martyn, published a paper entitled *Hints on Aerostatic Globes*, in which he included a theoretical design for a navigable balloon fitted with sails, a rudder, and beneath it 'an Umbrella to afford an easy descent, should the balloon burst', which he claimed was similar to one he had shown to the Prince of Wales the year before.

A fiasco of an attempt to make a parachute descent from a balloon occurred in 1785, when another Englishman, Stuart Amos Arnold, a former naval purser, rose from St George's Parade, London in the balloon *Royal George*, which had an open silk parachute fixed beneath it. On a large flat basket under the parachute lay Arnold's assistant, George Appleby, who according to advance publicity would drop from a mile above the earth. Disaster overtook the project only seconds after launching. The balloon hit some railings and lurched into the sky without Appleby and Arnold senior, but with Arnold's son. The balloon, which was over-inflated, burst, and the envelope shot up into the net, slowing the descent. The boy was thrown out into the Thames otherwise unharmed. For the first time, but not the last, a parachute had been created by the balloon itself.

In France, more was being heard of the balloonist Jean-Pierre Blanchard, a man whose personality was less impressive than some of his achievements. He was courageous but also had streaks of vanity, jealousy and, when it suited him, deceitfulness. Blanchard was born in Normandy in 1753 to poor parents, and although he received little education he did have a natural talent for mechanical inventions. He is said to have built a mechanical carriage and travelled in it at the age of six, devised a rat trap and constructed a velocipede – a primitive bicycle – at sixteen, and at twenty-nine to have made an elaborate device for raising the waters of the Seine. For a balloon ascent from Paris on 27 February 1784, Blanchard fitted a parachute over the car, but this, combined with the wings and rudder, was more than the balloon could manage. Five days later he made his first ascent from the Champ de Mars without them. For his next trip, he went up in an air balloon from Paris carrying paddles, in theory to push himself along, and a rudder for steering – both useless frills, as is now generally recognised.

Blanchard revived his interest in parachutes when he visited England in 1784 and 1785. He quarrelled with Thomas Martyn, whose paper on aerostatic globes contained a design for a balloon with an umbrella attachment, and through the press sent Martyn a mocking letter claiming that he himself had invented the device, adding disdainfully: 'As to its being adapted to air balloons, let the discovery be yours: experience has convinced me that it can answer no manner of purpose.' Martyn merely replied that the only originality he claimed was the parachute's adaptation to balloon use. On 3 June 1785, Blanchard experimented with a silk parachute 20ft (6m) in diameter dropped from a balloon above his much-vaunted but short-lived Balloon and Parachute Aerostatic Academy in Vauxhall. Two weeks later he tried to repeat the experiment with a sheep, but the demonstration failed and he was forced to give frustrated spectators their money back. In subsequent experiments he used a dog as a passenger, then two years later made a parachute large enough to suspend a man or large animal, though there is doubt as to whether he had faith enough to try it out himself.

Blanchard was fond of dropping animals on parachutes. This contemporary account, published in the *Journal de Paris* in 1785, describes his ascent from Lille on 26 August of that year and gives a fascinating glimpse of the hero worship accorded to the early aeronauts, particularly a publicity-conscious fellow like Blanchard:

> Monsieur Blanchard had completed the filling of the balloon at 9.45 a.m., and he then applied himself to the various preparations for the departure and the testing of the parachute. At 10.45 he entered the car with the Chevalier de l'Épinard, at which juncture the people who were assembled on the esplanade – the point of departure – cheered and applauded heartily.
>
> At 10.55 a.m. the ropes were cut and the balloon rose majestically into the sky. The aeronauts waved to the onlookers with their flags on which the arms of the town were painted. The balloon travelled southwards as it ascended, the wind being north-westerly. After four minutes the balloon was seen to sink a few fathoms and rise as quickly. At this point Monsieur Blanchard released the parachute, to which a dog was fastened, which seemed to fall very slowly; the dog came down three quarters of a league [3.6km] from the town, quite unharmed ... The

balloon was in sight for three quarters of an hour . . . There is no need to describe the feelings of the public at the moment that the balloon lifted off; they differed in no way from those of all men in sensibility.

A lavish reception and even more substantial rewards were in store for the pair:

M Blanchard and the Chevalier de l'Épinard came down at 6 p.m. at Senon in the region of Clermont. The next day they repaired to Sainte Menehould. The Municipal Officers, who had been informed of their impending arrival by a letter from the two aeronauts, welcomed them at the gates of the town, accompanied by the Knights of the Arquebus in full armour. They presented an honorary draught of wine to the two gentlemen and invited them to go down to the Town Hall where food and drink were awaiting them. They were led through a throng of cheering citizens to the Hall, where they dined.

The Magistrates of Lille, felicitating MM Blanchard and l'Épinard on their aerial voyage when they went down into town, entered a record of the event in the registers. M Blanchard had been granted the sum of 1,200 pounds French on his departure; they issued an order that he be granted a similar sum for his return, unless he prefer a box of gold decorated with the insignia of the town, of the same value and with a suitable inscription. As for the Chevalier de l'Épinard, the Magistrates reserved the right to offer him a gift.

A courageous attempt at parachute jumping is reported to have been made a few years later by an Englishman named Murray in Portsmouth, where he is reported to have thrown himself off a church tower and come down unharmed. Encouraged by this, he tried the same thing from the Bell Tower of Chichester Cathedral, with less success. About 14ft (4.2m) from the top he was caught by a gust of wind which blew him and his parachute alongside each other in mid-air. He managed to right himself, but the wind caught him again and he fell to the ground, blood gushing from his ears, nose and mouth. Whether he survived or not is not known, but he was unconscious for hours.

By the time Blanchard was ready to make his epic balloon trip across the Channel from Dover to Calais in January 1785, he had abandoned carrying a parachute on the grounds of weight and apparent uselessness. Blanchard's companion and sponsor was

Dr John Jeffries, an American. Jeffries's presence was rather resented by Blanchard – a strange attitude towards a sponsor, but he probably begrudged sharing any kudos in the event of triumph. Blanchard thought of several reasons why the American should remain on the ground, one of which was that the balloon could not carry more than one person in addition to its ballast. Blanchard was not above trickery to prove his point, even to the extent of filling his pockets with lead to increase his weight artificially. Even when Jeffries discovered this, he charitably bore Blanchard no ill will, but accompanied him as if nothing untoward had happened. A combination of bad piloting and a probable leak in the balloon aroused fears for the couple's safety. So unresponsive was it early in its flight that ballast and everything else was eventually jettisoned to lighten the burden. By the time they had made landfall in the Forest of Guînes, clothing, anchors, 'steering gear', ornaments, oars, wings, and even Jeffries's jacket and Blanchard's trousers, had been thrown overboard. And with them, presumably, went some of Blanchard's over-developed sense of pride.

Chapter Two

Triumphs and a Tragedy

In 1783, it is reported, a French general named Bournonville was sent by the National Convention with four companions to begin negotiations with the Prince of Saxe-Coburg. Without warning, all five were seized and imprisoned in the fortress of Olmutz. Determined to escape, Bournonville jumped with an umbrella from a window 40ft (12m) up, fell, breaking his leg, and was rewarded with another spell behind bars. Whether this story is true or not, such hesitant early steps with umbrellas, parachutes and dropping of animals as cargo with them were soon to lengthen into strides. We owe that to another Frenchman, André-Jacques Garnerin, who scored a historic first above what is today the Parc Monceau in Paris. To him falls the honour of being the first aeronaut to drop from a balloon by parachute and land alive.

Garnerin's first ascent had taken place in 1787 from Metz, but he later opposed the King in the French Revolution, checking his aeronautical career in mid-flight, so to speak. He had been sent by his government as a Special Commissioner to the Army of the North, was taken prisoner and confined in a fortress in Bude, Hungary, for three years. Here, Citizen Garnerin began toying with thoughts of escape by parachute, as he explained in the programme for his great Paris descent of 22 October 1797:

> The love of liberty so naturally gave rise to many projects to release myself from the rigorous detention. To surprise the vigilance of the sentries, force walls 10ft [3m] thick, throw myself from the ramparts without being injured, were schemes that afforded recreation. Blanchard's idea of presenting large surfaces to the air to increase its resistance, and the known acceleration of movement in all falling bodies, appeared to me only to require a careful mathematical comparison to be employed with certain success. I applied myself to the problem.

22

After deciding on the size of the parachute for descending from a rampart or a precipice, by natural sequence I devised the size and form of a parachute for a descent of several thousand feet by an aeronaut.

Garnerin's dream of escape from prison, hardly realistic in the circumstances, came to naught, but he was determined to make a parachute jump after his release. His October 1797 jump was made with a parachute shaped like an umbrella, of thirty-two ribbed segments of white canvas and 23ft (7m) in diameter when open. At the top there was a flat disc of wood to which were hinged the parachute ribs, and four feet (1.2m) below this a wooden hoop eight feet (2.4m) in diameter from which hung the long skirt of the rest of the parachute. The whole assemblage was attached to the net of Garnerin's balloon by means of a central pole, like an umbrella handle, which poked into an aperture at the top. Garnerin himself was to travel in a basket underneath. Like most other pioneers challenging the unknown, Garnerin was not short of courage. He conducted his experiment, with himself as the willing guinea-pig, entirely alone; any credit for its success would belong to him, any blame for failure would attach – even if posthumously – to him too, for the parachute was fashioned to his own design.

Fortunately, his self-confidence was justified, but at times it seemed a close-run thing because the parachute oscillated violently on its way down. A contemporary account, describing the scene in the Parc Monceau, noted that a 'deep silence reigned in the assembly and anxiety showed on all faces. When he reached a height of 3,000ft [915m] he cut the cords which held the parachute to the balloon . . . the latter exploded and the parachute began to descend with such rapidity that a cry of horror escaped from the spectators and several ladies fainted'. Nevertheless, Garnerin reached the ground safely, mounted a horse and rode back to the park and a 'stormy ovation'. Many years later, a noted compatriot, Charles Dollfus, founder of the Musée de l'Air in Paris and one of the world's leading balloonists, described Garnerin's deed as 'one of the great acts of heroism in human history'. If this sounds a trifle extravagant, consider that at that time Garnerin was making a leap into the unknown: the sky for jumping in was uncharted territory. Garnerin's chronicler noted the 'rapidity' of the parachute's descent, but at a 23ft (7m) flying diameter, Garnerin's parachute was a good deal bigger than, say, the RAF's

emergency version which had a flying diameter of around 16ft
(4.8m). But one unhappy by-product of the Frenchman's drops
was the oscillation, which would always cause him sickness. This
highlights an important aspect of a parachute canopy's efficiency:
porosity. Garnerin's parachute was made of canvas, and so far less
porous than a twentieth-century wartime pilot's silk or nylon one,
which allowed air to flow evenly through the fabric. Air would
have spilled out of the sides of Garnerin's parachute, as it had
an insufficient aperture to allow enough air to escape, hence the
instability.

Amazingly for this period, there were also a number of plucky
women who had taken to the air. One was Garnerin's own wife,
Jeanne Geneviève. Two years after her husband's first jump, she
added to her reputation as the world's first woman balloonist by
also becoming the first woman to use a parachute. Garnerin's
niece Elisa was also to make a name for herself as a professional
parachutist: between 1815 and 1836 she made thirty-nine drops.

The scene for Garnerin's fifth parachute jump, the first in
Britain, was London. Enjoying a brief respite in the Napoleonic
Wars granted by the Peace of Amiens in March 1802, the English
were for once rather better disposed towards the French – some of
them, at any rate – and particularly towards a man such as Garnerin,
who had star quality. So, on the evening of 21 September 1802,
excited Londoners paid five shillings (25p) each, a goodly sum
in those days, to watch the spectacle. It took place at St George's
Parade in North Audley Street, across Oxford Street from where
Selfridges stands today. Interest had spread far beyond the Parade
ground. One observer thought it had attracted the biggest crowds
London had ever seen, with people filling the streets as far afield as
Temple Bar in the Strand to the east and Primrose Hill, just to the
north of Regent's Park. Pot-boys from nearby public houses were
kept busy climbing up with jugs of porter, pipes and tobacco for
the spectators, who so massed on the specially erected scaffolding
that there were fears for their safety. Sightseers anxious to miss
nothing clambered up to every accessible vantage point, even
sitting astride gabled housetops and clinging to chimney stacks.

On this clear autumn evening, only the merest south-westerly
breeze stirred the treetops. By 5.14 p.m. Garnerin's huge striped
balloon had been filled with hydrogen and the delicate process of
attaching the parachute began. The sides of the canvas canopy, as
it hung from the balloon, were about 15ft (4.5m) long, tied to an 8ft
(2.4m) hoop whose upper part formed a surface like a drumhead,

with a circular aperture of 1½ ft (0.5m) in the middle. Attached to the aperture was a tube containing a rope connected to the balloon. Women spectators were amused to note that, hanging as it did in folds, the parachute resembled a hooped petticoat. Under the parachute, the imperturbable Monsieur Garnerin fixed the small cylindrical basket, a mere four feet (1.2m) high and two and a quarter feet (0.7m) in diameter, the cords from the parachute hem and those from the basket being gathered in a firm knot above his head. During these preparations some of the crowd became restive and over-eager, and the jostling round the basket almost made Garnerin and his assistant lose patience. Eventually, all was ready, and Garnerin climbed in, dressed in a blue jacket, white waistcoat and nankeen pantaloons, and by this time well-primed with porter. It was an impressive scene. There were crowds as far as the eye could see, with the balloon and parachute together totalling 120ft (36m) in height as the centrepiece.

For some time before the ascent, noted a newspaper reporter with a fanciful turn of phrase, pigeons kept flying about the balloon and 'appeared frequently disposed to perch on it as if to greet the entrance of man into their element'. The shouting grew, the last rope was cut, and at 5.45 p.m. the mighty structure glided upwards, with Garnerin leaning from his basket and waving to the multitude with his silk French tricolour. Here is Garnerin's own account in a contemporary translation into English from the *Annual Visitor.*

> I suspended my parachute to the balloon. This painful and difficult operation was executed with all possible address by the assistance of the most distinguished personages. The parachute was gradually suspended, and the breeze, which was very gentle, did not produce the least obstacle. At length I hastened to ballast my bark, and to place myself in it: a sight which the public contemplated with deep interest – it seemed at that moment as if every heart beat in unison for, although I have not the advantage of speaking English, everyone understands my signs. I ascertained the height of the barometer, which was 29½in [75cm]. I now pressed the moment of my departure and the period of fulfilling my engagements with the British public.
>
> All the cords were cut. I arose amidst the most impressive silence . . . and discovered from on high the countless multitude that sent up sighs and prayers for my safety. I quickened my ascending impulse and rose through light and thin vapours,

where the cold air informed me that I was entering the upper region . . .

I examined my barometer, which I found had fallen to 23 inches [58cm]. The sky was clear, the moment favourable, and I threw down my flag to show the people assembled that I was on the point of cutting the cord that suspended me between heaven and earth. I made every necessary disposition, prepared my ballast and measured with my eye the vast space that separated me from the rest of the human race . . . I then took out my knife with a hand firm from a conscience void of reproach, and which had never been lifted against anyone but in the field of victory, and cut the cord. My balloon rose, and I felt myself precipitated with a velocity which was checked by the sudden unfolding of my parachute. I saw that all my calculations were correct, and my mind remained calm and serene. I endeavoured to modulate my gravitation, and the oscillation which I experienced increased in proportion as I approached the breeze that blows in the middle regions: nearly ten minutes had elapsed, and I felt that the more time I took in descending the safer I should reach the ground.

At length I perceived thousands of people, some on horseback, others on foot, following me, all of whom encouraged me by their wishes, while they opened their arms to receive me. I came near the earth, and after one bound, I landed and quitted the parachute without shock or accident. The first person who came to me pressed me in his arms; but without losing any time, I employed myself in detaching the principal circle of the parachute, anxious to save the instrument that had so well guaranteed me, but a crowd soon surrounded me – laid hold of me, and carried me in triumph, till an indisposition, the consequence and effect of the oscillation I had experienced, obliged me to stop.

I was then seized with a painful vomiting, which I usually experience for several hours after a descent in a parachute. The interval of a moment, however, permitting me to get on horseback, a numerous cavalcade approached to keep off the crowd, whose enthusiasm and transport incommoded me not a little. The Duke of York was amongst the horsemen, and the procession proceeded with great difficulty in the midst of the crowd, who shouted their applause, and had before the Tricolour which I had thrown down and which was carried by a Member of Parliament . . .

At length, after several incidents, all produced by the universal interest with which I was honoured, I withdrew from the crowd without any other accident than that of having my right foot jammed between the horse I rode and a horseman who pressed too close . . .

My parachute was preserved as well as could be expected, a few of the cords only were cut – it is now exhibited at the Pantheon, where a great concourse of persons have been to examine it.

In the ten minutes that Garnerin was in the air, spectators at St George's Parade saw him almost disappear from view to a height of about 8,000ft (2,440m). He cut himself and the parachute loose when the balloon was above Tottenham Court Road. Garnerin's account was not an exaggeration. As the parachute lurched earthwards in a field behind St Pancras Church, it was seen to sway violently, the Frenchman being 'tossed from side to side like the pendulum of a clock', reported one onlooker. The oscillation was said to be far worse than it had been in Paris five years before. When Garnerin landed, he was certainly sick, as always, but he recovered sufficiently to dispense handshakes to applauding well-wishers, several of whom ran up to the parachute and tore strips of coloured paper off the basket for souvenirs. The Duke of York's presence at the descent was a nice piece of irony, for he it was who commanded the Austrian division which had taken Garnerin prisoner some years earlier. Also there was Lord Stanhope, on foot, 'from whom I received the counsels of a scientific man, and who penetrated the crowd to shake hands with me'.

If Garnerin was once again high in public favour, parachuting itself was not. Several newspapers admonished the public for supporting the event and also, by implication, Garnerin for initiating it. The *Sun*, a London evening paper of the time, wrote: 'This is the first experiment of the kind in this Country, and we sincerely hope it will be the last. We mean not to detract from the skill and the courage displayed by M. Garnerin upon this occasion; indeed it would be impossible if we were so inclined; but the man who could feel any pleasure in seeing the life of his fellow creature exposed to such imminent danger, without any adequate cause, must possess either the most unidentifiable curiosity, or the most brutal apathy'. In retrospect, nearly two centuries on, this view does seem harsh. Pioneers deserve and appreciate, but do not always receive, the interest and support of the public. These were early days in aeronautics. We have to remember that ballooning had not yet entered its century-long heyday, Sir George Cayley's development of true winged flight was still in its infancy, and parachute jumping from balloons was a novelty. Some of the crowd may have come for the thrill of a tragedy, much as spectators gather at a jump in the hope of seeing a horse take a tumble. But there was genuine admiration among the crowd here. This is what one eyewitness wrote: 'As the parachute came near the earth the swinging motion increased, and many turned their eyes away from the terror of beholding an entire upset and the consequent destruction of the aeronaut. The distress was universal . . . and for the honour of British humanity there was not one who would not have purchased the assurance of his safety, almost any price.' A genuine enough tribute.

Now there was another pioneer-to-be among Garnerin's watchers. He was a twenty-five-year-old watercolour painter, amateur scientist and ballooning enthusiast named Robert Cocking, whose attention was particularly caught by the Frenchman's nauseous journey down. He resolved to solve this problem and was to spend years studying parachutes in an attempt to arrive at a stable design. At first he thought Garnerin's oscillation might be cured by using an unlikely-sounding system of adjustable weights mounted to slide on rods. He then hit on the idea of a parachute shaped like an inverted cone, like a saucer, having one day observed, it is said, that a parasol which fell handle downwards from a balcony hit the ground with the stick uppermost. This strange cone shape could also have been an echo of a parachute designed by Cayley, recognised today as the father of aeronautics and the true inventor of the aeroplane. In February 1810, seven years after Garnerin's London descent, he wrote an article condemning Garnerin's parachute as being 'nearly the worst possible'. In Cayley's view, based on his observations of the goat's-beard plant, the seeds of which are wafted away on small dihedral 'parachutes', the inverted cone shape was preferable. It was to be many years, though, before Cocking could put a modified version to the test. He simply could not afford to.

After 1802, parachuting continued apace abroad. On 24 July 1808, a Polish balloonist, Jordaki Kuparento, ascended from Warsaw in a balloon that caught fire and forced him to make the first life-saving jump with a parachute. We know little about this event, and some claim that it did not happen at all, but we do know that within a few years parachutes were being used, along with rockets, in war. In Britain, Col William Congreve, in a book published for the information of officers in the Rocket Corps, included a description of a forty-two-pounder (19kg) light ball or floating carcass rocket containing a parachute flare, which could burn for ten minutes and had a range of one and three quarter miles (2.4km).

The year 1819 was notable for two events. Louis-Charles made the first parachute jump in America from a balloon 500ft (152m) above Jersey City, and there was tragedy for the Blanchard family, with a parachute the indirect cause. Jean-Pierre's wife Magdeleine, a noted woman balloonist, solo professional and a rival of Garnerin's niece Elisa, was taking part in an exhibition balloon ascent involving fireworks at the Tivoli Gardens in Paris. Four hundred feet (122m) up, her balloon aglow with fizzing fire, she sent down 'bombs' of silver rain on little parachutes. Suddenly, to the crowd's horror, the balloon caught fire and the blazing envelope sank quickly to earth, throwing Mme Blanchard to her death among the rooftops of the Rue de Provence. The cause of the fire is thought to have been a down-draught of gas from the balloon's neck coming into contact with the wand she used to touch off the fireworks.

In England, references to parachutes appeared sporadically in the press. In May 1826 a reader of *Mechanics' Magazine,* signing himself 'Daedalus', suggested copying parachutes from nature, using as models the airborne seeds of syngenesious plants. His suggestion for the best form of parachute was 'that of a wheel, from the centre of which should be suspended a pole of adequate length . . . The spokes of this wheel should be made of the lightest materials. Between them, large and strong feathers might be fixed in holes prepared to receive them in the cane . . . the whole would then form a machine resembling the winged down of plants.' Experiments, added 'Daedalus' prudently, should start on a small scale before man-sized ones were made.

For many years no parachute jumps were attempted in England. Robert Cocking was still nursing his idea of an inverted cone parachute after Garnerin's 1802 jump in London, but was certainly in no position to put it to the test. As a painter he was not a commercial success, so he had to be content with experimenting with models, dropping them from high points such as the Monument in the City of London and on Hampstead Heath. But for an opportunity to turn theory into fact he had to wait thirty-five years, until 1837. He was then sixty-one years old.

At this time a great new balloon, the *Royal Vauxhall*, had been made for the use of Charles Green, the most famous aeronaut of the day. Green was to be remembered for two developments, apart from his ballooning exploits: the introduction of coal gas in 1821 as a cheaper, if less buoyant, substitute for hydrogen as a lifting agent, and the use of a trail-rope for a balloon to drag along the ground to provide automatic ballast for low-level flights. Green's was a huge colourful new balloon fashioned out of more than 2,000 yards (1,830m) of crimson and white silk. In November 1836, the balloon and its pilot had figured in a notable marathon trip. With two passengers – Robert Hollond MP, sponsor of the flight, and Monck Mason, a leading aeronautics expert – they rose from Vauxhall Gardens, glided over southern England, crossed the Channel and landed in a field near Weilberg in the Duchy of Nassau (now part of Germany) eighteen hours and 480 miles (772km) later, a distance record which was to hold for seventy-one years.

Only a balloon of the stature and lifting power of the *Royal Vauxhall* (now renamed the *Nassau*) was likely to bear Cocking's parachute. This was not yet made, and lacking the resources to build it himself, he had to turn to others. After much thought he went along to Vauxhall Gardens, near Millbank in London, a favourite ballooning venue whose proprietors also owned the *Royal Nassau* balloon. Cocking offered a deal: if they financed the cost of making his parachute, he would provide what he fondly hoped would be a spectacular performance free of charge. And so the great saucer took shape, a huge device fashioned out of Irish linen with ribs and braces, 33ft (10m) in diameter, with paintings decorating its underside. Framing the parachute at its perimeter was a metal hoop 107ft (32.5m) in circumference. The whole contrivance weighed 223lb (101kg), added to which was Cocking's own weight of 170lb (77kg), a total of around 400lb (181kg).

Cocking could hardly have engaged a more capable balloonist than Green, who was, however, anxious about the risk involved in any great upward thrust of the balloon which might follow the release of Cocking and the parachute, and he feared for Cocking because the parachute had not been tested using a dead weight. Fearing to release Cocking himself, in case he should be blamed for any mishap, Green said he would prefer not to cut the parachute free, but preferred to install a so-called 'liberating mechanism' for Cocking to use to release himself. There were doubts about the strength of the parachute's tin-tubing frame, which Cocking's friends felt would have been stronger made of ash. But Cocking was in no mood for objections. The whole design and execution, he maintained, had been approved by scientists and was therefore ideal, and posters advertising the descent made confident references to the 'unerring principles' on which the parachute was constructed. But Monck Mason, the aeronautics expert, was also pessimistic, so much so that at two o'clock in the morning of the day announced for the descent, Monday, 24 July 1837, he sent a long and gloomy letter to the *Morning Herald*. Arriving too late to be published in full, it was heavily cut and unfortunately the impact of its message was lost. This paragraph was among those omitted: 'I have no hesitation in predicting that one of two events must inevitably take place ... either [the parachute] will come to the ground with a degree of force we have before shown to be incompatible with the final preservation of the individual, or should it be attempted to make it sufficiently light to resist this conclusion it must give way beneath the undue exercise of force which will necessarily develop in the descent ...' In short, the parachute would be too heavy or too flimsy for Cocking to survive. Cocking was unconcerned, however; not for a moment did he countenance any possibility of failure, and he told observers so in no uncertain terms.

So in Vauxhall Gardens, into the balloon's car climbed the grimly hopeful Charles Green and his companion Edward Spencer. Below them, in the parachute's wicker basket, stood the confident, determined figure of Cocking, a short stout figure in striped satin jacket and white trousers, waving cheerfully to the crowds. The band of the Surrey Yeomanry struck up the National Anthem and at around 7.30 p.m. to the accompaniment of cheering and clapping from the spectators, the balloon drifted in stately fashion upwards into the gentle north-west wind.

Almost immediately, a complication arose. Two hundred feet (61m) from the ground, the balloon lost the cloth tube carefully provided to pour ballast away from the parachute's bowl, and Green and Spencer had to throw it clear as well as they could by hand. Cocking had hoped to release himself at 8,000ft (2,440m), but the balloon, now drifting slowly south-eastwards, could not gain height quickly enough – a sign, perhaps, that the combined weight of parachute and passenger was beginning to tell. Green commented later:

As soon as we had attained the height of five thousand feet [1,525m] I told him that it would be impossible for us to get up as high as he desired in sufficient time for him to descend by the light of day. Upon this, Mr Cocking said, 'Then I shall very soon leave you. But tell me whereabouts I am.' Mr Spencer replied, 'We appear to be on a level with Greenwich.' Spencer asked him if he felt himself quite comfortable, and whether he found that the practical trial bore out the calculations he had made. Mr Cocking said, 'Yes, I never felt more comfortable or more delighted in my life.' Shortly afterwards Mr Cocking said, 'Well, now I think I shall leave you.' I answered, 'I wish you a very good night and a safe descent, if you are determined to make it and not to use the tackle.'

The 'tackle' was some apparatus rigged by Frederick Gye, manager of the Vauxhall Gardens, and Green to help Cocking up into the balloon basket if he had a last-minute change of mind about making the jump. Cocking disdained the chance to withdraw and said simply, 'Good night Spencer, good night Green,' and tugged at the liberating mechanism. The first attempt failed, then with a powerful jerk Cocking released it whereupon, according to Green, the balloon, now freed of its burden, 'shot upwards with the velocity of a sky-rocket':

> The effect upon us at this moment is almost beyond description. The immense machine which suspended us between heaven and earth, whilst it appeared to be forced upwards with terrific violence and rapidity through unknown and untravelled regions, amidst the howlings of a fearful hurricane, rolled about as though revelling in a freedom for which it had long struggled . . . Gas was rushing in torrents from the upper and lower valves . . . Had it not been for the application to our mouths of two pipes leading into an air bag with which we had furnished ourselves previous to starting, we must within a minute have been suffocated, and so, but by different means, have shared the melancholy fate of our friend.

Hardly had poor Cocking cut himself free of the balloon when the fears of so many sceptics were proved justified. To the accompaniment of crackling wood and crumpling tin, the parachute canopy and its framework collapsed, and Cocking plummeted to earth with the swaying mass of debris miles from where the crowds had cheered him on his way. He was found among the wreckage on Burnt Ash Hill, near Lee in south-east London, so badly injured that he died within minutes. So perished the ageing parachute pioneer Robert Cocking. Over-confident he may have been, but he deserved better than the sequel to the tragedy. Shortly afterwards, his body and the remains of the parachute were taken to the Tiger's Head public house nearby. There, on the floor, they were exhibited to the public in a degrading peepshow, the body and the parachute each at sixpence (2½p) a time, tickets being provided in the bar. Only after protests from Mr Gye, manager of Vauxhall Gardens, was it banned by a magistrate. Today, Robert Cocking's grave can still be seen in the old churchyard opposite St. Margaret's Church at Lee, a sad memorial whose stone was erected by an anonymous 'fellow aeronaut' some seventy years later.

A month after Cocking's death, Mrs George Graham, a balloonist herself as well as the wife of one, took part at Hackney in a benefit exhibition in aid of Cocking's widow. She ascended in the *Royal Victoria* balloon and from the basket dropped two model parachutes, one of the Garnerin type and one resembling Cocking's inverted cone. It was the latter that made the better descent. The American aeronaut John Wise, who was in his third year of parachuting, was also curious about the Cocking tragedy. Three months afterwards he too compared the Cocking and Garnerin parachutes. Wise took his balloon up at Philadelphia bearing a couple of test parachutes and released them at 2,500ft (625m), his dog Tray in the basket of the Garnerin type and his cat Tabitha borne by the Cocking. The first oscillated wildly like its full-sized predecessor, but the Cocking version came down safely, if rotating slightly.

So what went wrong with Cocking's real parachute? It seems strange that if his model design emerged as the more stable of the two, that his should actually fail so completely. It is, of course, uncertain whether the experimenters were making true comparisons size for size, fabric for fabric, weight for weight. The question was considered in the Royal Aeronautical Society's *Journal* in 1962 by the late Sidney Jackson, chief designer of Irvin Air Chute of Great Britain (now Irvin Aerospace), makers of the emergency parachute for the RAF for many years from the 1920s. Garnerin's parachute fabric, Jackson pointed out, was completely impervious to air – in today's terminology, it had nil porosity. This, coupled with the flattish shape of the canopy, would not be inclined to give good stability. At that time, he observed, there was 'almost a complete failure to comprehend the problem'. Contemporary commentators on the Cocking experience were equally in the dark, according to Jackson: 'It is almost certain . . . that Cocking's parachute failed for purely structural reasons.' The fact is that Cocking resisted all pressure to strengthen the parachute during construction. 'Don't let me have it so heavy,' he said when Mr Gye and the proprietors of Vauxhall Gardens urged the strengthening of the tin-tube frame.

A year after Cocking's death, John Poole, a popular author of the day, wrote a book called *Crotchets in the Air* which described a balloon trip with Charles Green. He wrote, *inter alia*: 'We all know the fate of that poor simpleton Cocking; so much for parachutes! . . . I entertain serious doubts as to whether parachutes, or firework ascents, can be rendered serviceable to science in any of its branches, unless coffin-making be reckoned of their number.' At that time, many members of the public would have agreed with him.

CHAPTER THREE

HAMPTON'S WINNING TRICK

S uch was the wave of indignation after Cocking's death that it seemed only the most determined of adventurers would risk public disapproval by making similar attempts at a successful parachute drop. But in the pages of the specialist journals, discussion was given over to remedy rather than remonstration.

The noted innovator Col Francis Maceroni, who in his time designed an armoured ship, paddle wheel and steam coach, wrote three weeks after the Cocking tragedy saying that he had experimented with weights and felt that, unlike Cocking's, 'the proper and perfectly efficacious construction for a parachute is similar to an umbrella; only, instead of whalebones or canes being brought to a point and attached to a stick, they must be attached to a ring or hoop of wood, of a diameter equal to one-fifth or one-quarter of the diameter of the parachute. Thus, there will be a large hole in the centre of the machine, through which compressed and accumulated air will rush and infallibly prevent its overturning, or even oscillating at all.' In 1804, claimed the Colonel, a man was seen by thousands to leap off the bridge in a place called La Tenità, which connected two streets by passing over another street, 122ft (37.2m) below. He himself had seen the man shortly afterwards. Fastened to his waist was an ordinary umbrella, but larger, and he reached the ground uninjured. This jumper had taken the precaution of fixing 'stays' all round the stick. (Col Maceroni, incidentally, had claimed that Garnerin's parachute had oscillated because the hole in the centre was no bigger than a man's hat.) In England, an architectural draughtsman, George Mackenzie, suggested a parachute equipped with a weight at the bottom of the rigging lines where the parachutists would normally be. The jumper would sit under the crown of the parachute where there would be a ring-shaped tube several feet wide, containing air.

Fifteen months after Robert Cocking's death, John Hampton,

aged thirty-nine, an erstwhile sailor turned professional balloonist, ignoring popular sentiment and the criticism of his friends, announced he would make a new attempt at a jump. Unlike Cocking, Hampton wanted to play safe with a parachute of orthodox design, modelled on Garnerin's of thirty-six years before. But there was one major difference: Garnerin's model unfolded after release from his balloon, while Hampton's was designed to have already opened out, like Cocking's. The canopy, made of stout gingham, was scalloped at the hem and measured 21ft (6.4m) in diameter when fully expanded on its 8ft (2.4m) ribs of whalebone. Sticks of bamboo connected the canopy to a hollow tube 11ft (3.4m) long, through which ran a rod with a wicker basket on the lower end.

Only a year had elapsed since Cocking's fatal jump, and it was still fresh in the mind. Hence, a few days before the jump, Hampton ran into trouble. While he was busy with preparations, it dawned on the owners of Montpellier Gardens, Cheltenham, where the descent was scheduled for 3 October 1838, that if the venture failed no small blame would fall on them for sanctioning it. Mr Spinney, manager of the gas works which had contracted to fill Hampton's balloon, sought local magistrates' guidance. Their worships, while admitting they had no legal powers to interfere with the project, sympathised with the protesters and suggested that if Mr Spinney refused to supply the balloonist with gas, a parachute jump would legally be prevented. Hampton argued hard, and was eventually allowed his gas on two conditions: that the ascent must be a 'captive' one, and that any parachute jump must be made within the Gardens. Reluctantly, Hampton went through the motions of keeping his part of the bargain.

In fact, Hampton's place in history as the first Englishman to make a parachute jump and survive was secured by a piece of trickery to beat the limitation of a tethered balloon ascent. When the day came, the balloon was inflated, the parachute attached beneath it, a large coil of strong rope hitched to the parachute basket, and the long end grasped firmly by twenty workmen who had been instructed to hold fast at all costs. But when the balloon and parachute were about 40ft (12.2m) above the ground, Hampton, who had been secretly abetted by his friend Granville Fletcher, produced a knife and quickly cut the tethering rope. The balloon rose to 8,000ft (2,440m), 1,000ft (305m) higher than he had originally planned. Once more the knife went to work,

36

this time to separate the parachute. 'My balloon ascended from me immediately after the separation, for some hundred feet,' reported Hampton later, 'and with a terrific noise rushed through the atmosphere, and in the space of a few seconds only, burst over my head with the violence of a thunder-bolt.'

Determined as he was to succeed, Hampton had not been wholly confident. During his balloon ascent he was seen to wave, not the customary Union Jack but, his audience was astonished to see, the Tricolour – the very one flourished by Garnerin in London in 1802. Three days later came the reason for this apparently eccentric gesture: 'It might be inquired why he did not rise under the standard of England,' wrote a fellow member of the Ancient Order of Druids in the *Cheltenham Free Press*. 'He would answer – though morally certain of success, an accident *might* occur, he *might* fail, and as an Englishman he was determined that in no event connected with him should an enterprise under the auspices of the British flag be sullied by defeat.' Hampton did not fail. His descent, lasting twelve minutes and forty seconds, was peacefully undisturbed by any dangerous oscillation, though on landing he did hit his head on an iron hoop used to strengthen the wicker basket, and cut himself above one eye.

The following year Hampton planned to ascend and jump again, this time from Cremorne Gardens, Chelsea, in London. Hampton, an aeronautical showman typical of his time, could never be accused of excessive modesty, as the wording on the poster shows:

> Mr Hampton, the unrivalled and intrepid Aeronaut, will have the honour to make his first appearance this Season at the above Splendid and Highly Distinguished Grounds, on Thursday, June 13, 1839, being his 15th Ascent with his Magnificent Balloon, the *Albion*, and at an Altitude of at least 1,000ft [3,050m] separate himself and Apparatus from the Balloon and descend in his Royal Safety Parachute. This truly enterprising and unparalleled feat having been successfully performed by Mr Hampton, last autumn, at Cheltenham, in the presence of an immense Assemblage of rank and Fashion, including upwards of 100,000 Spectators!!!

Thursday, 13 June turned out to be dangerously windy. Considering the prospects in Cremorne Gardens, Hampton knew as he glanced round the great crowds pouring in that he could never clear the nearby trees. He decided to call off the ascent, but the crowd, many of whom seemed more interested in spills than thrills, demanded their money back. Hampton tried to persuade them to come back next day, but they would have none of it. Reluctantly, and against his better judgement, he released the balloon and went through with the parachute jump. The parachute descended at a 'frightful speed', according to witnesses, and the horseman who galloped off to look for Hampton found him at Walham Green, injured after landing up against a wall. The cords on his parachute had become entangled, hampering control. The newspapers of the day were still disdainful of the lower orders who sought their pleasure in other people's risks: 'The bravery, or temerity, of Mr Hampton may perhaps excite admiration in some breasts, and in many, pity,' wrote one reporter, 'but the cold-blooded inhumanity of the brawling sightseers cannot otherwise be regarded than with a unanimous feeling of detestation.' And the *Mechanics' Magazine* wrote: 'Were these ascents and descents made by way of experiment with a view to testing any scientific fact, or for the investigation of any natural phenomenon, we of course would not properly object to them, but made as mere exhibitions to gratify the excited appetites of a mob of gazers, we must cordially agree in the just condemnation given to them.'

As a professional exhibitionist, Hampton was a first-class salesman for himself and his skill as a performer, but he was also given to a salesman's economy with the truth. For example, he grossly overstated the dangers of parachuting by saying that drops through the air made breathing difficult. This is simply not so, and the effect was to discourage experimenting with any parachute without a rigid framework; a loose-canopied one would, it was thought, produce a fall so rapid as to induce unconsciousness, a complete misconception that was to persist for at least another eighty years.

So it was the heyday of the showman rather than the experimenter. Along with concerts, theatrical firework displays, circus turns, pony racing, gymnastics, singing and dancing, or simply taking tea in the company of friends, balloon ascents and the occasional parachute jump became accepted features of London's outdoor entertainment. Aeronautical feats became increasingly bizarre to match a crowd's appetite for novelty and excitement. Charles Green, the serious pioneer and famous balloonist who had grudgingly facilitated Cocking's foolhardy jump beneath the *Nassau* balloon, was one day reduced to the indignity of ascending in his balloon on horseback. On another occasion he took up a woman and a leopard as passengers. But Green was also a serious aeronaut. To him, in 1850, goes the credit for devising the first parachute supply-dropping system. This was in an effort to save Sir John Franklin, who had disappeared in the Arctic in 1847. Green made a balloon of about thirty cubic feet capacity and capable of drifting up to 600 miles, under which he attached packets and parachutes for carrying food and messages. The intention was to release them automatically by means of a slow-burning match. Whether the drop was actually made or not is not known, but the bodies of Franklin and his colleagues were found twelve years after they disappeared.

At this time, most serious jumpers played safe with traditional parachute designs, but occasionally an experimenter came along. A new kind of parachute contraption made its début in London in June 1854 when Henri Letur, a diminutive forty-eight-year-old French circus performer, brought over a large umbrella-shaped canopy beneath which were treadle-driven wings which flapped fifty times a minutes. Letur had made about thirty accident-free trips with it in France, three of them over the Champs-Elysées before the emperor and empress. While unable to take off from the ground unaided, he could make a regulated and safe descent. His first attempt in London, from Cremorne Gardens, took him to Blackheath, where he literally dropped in to see some friends after a descent which lasted three quarters of an hour. His second, on 27 June beneath W. H. Adams's balloon, was fatal. The Frenchman, a slightly deformed figure prematurely aged by years of circus turns, had laughed off spectators' pessimism, and certainly the lift-off was smooth enough. But as balloon and jumper swung away to the north-east on the south-west wind, Adams realised above Camden Town that one of the supporting ropes to Letur's device was twisted. Unable to speak French, he could not warn Letur, who in turn could not understand English. Over open countryside at Tottenham, he cut two of the three ropes, leaving the third still entangled with one of the wings. Adams put the balloon down slowly, but the wind caught it and blew it across a field and through trees with considerable violence. Poor Letur was seriously injured and, with blood pouring down his face, lay where he fell, moaning simply '*Mon Dieu, mon Dieu*' until he was taken to hospital, where he died eight days later. At his inquest, several jurors called for a letter to be sent to the Secretary of State urging that similar parachute descents should be banned. The majority, however, felt that this would only obstruct the progress of science.

The antics of some performers in the aeronautical 'circus' around this time incurred the outspoken disapproval, possibly inspired by professional pique, of John Hampton, who had by now given up his parachuting career after only seven jumps. He expressed himself in print, seizing in particular upon a French couple, the Poitevins, who had staged numerous balloon ascents in France with animals, including a bull. They also came to England. In the *Morning Herald* on 6 September 1852, Hampton attacked first their 'brutal system' of animal ascents, which he described as 'torture . . . with impunity'. Then his anger turned upon Monsieur Poitevin alone. 'Now this bold and courageous husband,' wrote Hampton acidly, 'intends to place his wife in the car of the parachute and for the gratification of vulgar taste, separate her from the balloon when at a great height.' He called on magistrates to stop the Frenchman's 'shameful propensities' and suggested that Monsieur Poitevin himself should make a jump, as Hampton had done fourteen years before. This sally had no effect whatever on the French pair. Madame Poitevin went up from Cremorne Gardens attached to her husband's balloon *Zodiac* and jumped with her parachute *Meteor* in perfect style from 5,000ft (1,525m), landing amid tremendous applause. Louise Poitevin was a good advertisement in the 1800s for the courage of her sex. She was a much-travelled parachutist and made at least thirty-five jumps throughout Europe, not at all deterred by several wet landings in the Mediterranean.

It was parachuting's increasing appearance before the public eye that prompted Sir George Cayley, the aeronautical innovator, to begin reiterating his ideas for so-called 'governable' parachutes. Despite his work for aeronautics, Cayley has been grossly under-rated. All most people recall at the mention of his name is that he sent up his coachman to test out a glider, who protested. His name never appeared in the *Dictionary of National Biography*, yet Charles Gibbs-Smith, the late aeronautical historian, has written: 'He is now seen to be the true inventor of the modern aeroplane – in the basic sense – and the founder of the science of aerodynamics applied to aircraft.' To Sir George, Gibbs-Smith attributes no fewer than twenty-eight aeronautical 'firsts'. In other fields, too, Cayley found outlets for his lively imagination: as inventor of the caterpillar tractor and a type of artificial mechanical limb. But aeronautics was his true milieu, and with astonishing prescience he foreshadowed today's highly manoeuvrable parachutes when he wrote to the *Mechanics' Magazine*: 'As the subject of parachutes again attracts public attention, permit me to suggest what would be an interesting addition to the mere hackneyed fact of their descent – their steerage from the moment they are liberated from the balloon to any desired landing-place, within about five to six times the distance horizontally that the balloon is then above the earth . . .' Cayley then described, with sketches, his plan for a navigable parachute. He envisaged a large wing with a dihedral angle stretched on a framework and shaped vaguely like a fish, with a car suspended beneath it. The whole structure, to be launched from a balloon, was actually not a parachute but a glider. Cayley, by that time aged seventy-nine, must have been bitterly disappointed that nobody considered his idea worth pursuing.

As in other fields, the Victorians were richly fecund in ideas. Even if practice did not always, or even often, measure up to theory, at least their optimism was impressive. Hugh Bell, a Londoner, in 1848 patented a sausage-shaped airship 56ft (17m) long, with propellers to be worked by hand and steering rudder behind. The balloon part was enclosed in flat silk bands for strength, and a single flat band fixed round its middle helped to convert it into a parachute in case of accident. Accompanying this was a device called a water grapnel, which could be dropped from a balloon into the sea; working on the same principle as the parachute, its collapsible 'umbrella' would unfold to act as a brake. Bell arranged trials in Vauxhall Gardens for his air vessel, but these were not a success.

With his silk bands idea, Bell may have been trying to reinforce a natural tendency for a torn balloon to form a parachute in any case. An impressive example of this occurred the previous year when four men endured one of the most frightening descents of all time. One of the Vauxhall balloons, Gypson's, was to make a night flight carrying 60lb (27kg) of fireworks, to be set off as part of a late-night entertainment over the Gardens. Youngest in the crew was Henry Coxwell, who later became a prominent aeronaut. The summer afternoon had been calm and hot, with prospects of a fine evening. Soon, however, clouds piled up, thunder rumbled in the distance and flashes of lightning lit up the London sky. After a hasty consultation among themselves the four decided that if the ascent were quick they could get up and down safely before the storm was upon them. So the balloon rose, with young Coxwell sitting on the hoop, ready to operate the valves. Minutes later the balloonists were thrilling the crowds with lavish festoons of Roman candles, petards and gold and silver rains. But 4,000ft (1,220m) up, they found themselves in the middle of the storm. The balloon, lightened of its fireworks, was rising fast. Coxwell sensed imminent danger, and said so, but he was ignored. 'If the valve is not opened, the balloon will burst!' warned Coxwell. Almost as he spoke, lightning flashed to reveal a 16ft (4.9m) gash in the balloon's envelope. With great presence of mind, Coxwell immediately cut the cord fastening the neck to the hoop of the fast-sinking balloon and, to their relief, the fabric leapt upwards to the limits of the net and spread out like a parachute, checking their fall. They came down, shaken but unharmed, in Pimlico.

The American balloonist John Wise had already carried out experiments along these lines in 1838. The first took place above Easton, Pennsylvania on 11 August. He intended to explode his balloon deliberately, but was forestalled – it did so by accident. The experiment worked, though; the lower part of the balloon misbehaved: the envelope was forced sideways instead of upwards. Wise came down heavily but unhurt.

Although many decades were to pass before the virtues of, and the need for, an efficient parachute became clear, suggestions for improvements to the existing framed parachute were not lacking. Back to nature was the message of William Bland of Hartlip, Kent, who after a Hampton parachute display wrote to *Mechanics' Magazine* maintaining that the parachute principle, as currently employed, was all wrong. And he sent the editor a box containing several 'most perfect and beautiful parachutes', actually the seeds, resembling flue-brushes, of a plant called stag's-horn fern (*Platycerium*). Another correspondent urged modelling the parachute on the convolvulus flower which, he observed, when thrown into the air always fell stalk first. Shades of Cocking . . .

It was the day of bizarre inventions, as complex as they were improbable. Most were doomed to be earthbound. John Henry Johnson, of Lincoln's Inn Fields, London, devised an elongated balloon with a platform suspended from it for aeronauts and machinery. There were to be steam-driven paddle-wheels 'for the purpose of counteracting the action of the air against the balloon', and parachute- or umbrella-shaped propellers sliding back and forth on horizontal rods, pushing the air back behind them and propelling the device along, guided by horizontal and vertical sails and a rudder. Another dreamer, Prosper Dartiguenave, chose a vertical system of steam-driven parachutes for his contraption, and 'when the desired elevation has been attained, I direct my machine by means of a horizontal flapper . . . My machine is also provided with wings, the better to enable it to turn and which can have their direction changed at the will of the aeronaut.' Perhaps fortunately for the inventor, notice to proceed with letters patent was not given within the prescribed time limit. One of the most eccentric of innovators was the Earl of Aldborough, who in 1855 patented a series of 'improvements' to aerial navigation. Page after page of the lengthy specification set out in astonishing detail an elaborate system of aerostats, many based on the parachute, for use in war. The drawings, resembling quaint variations of large paper darts, were so vague, however, that it was difficult to imagine exactly what the noble lord was striving for. This did not prevent him drawing up plans, many times amended in subsequent years, for a series of fortified ports, landing places or harbours for his warlike aerial vessels. And another hopeful inventor patented a balloon with flapping wings, based on the flap-valve principle, these valves opening on the upstroke and closing on the down with the object of achieving lift. The wings, when still, would be used like a parachute to make the descent, as he put it, 'quite free from danger'.

A Montgolfier hot-air balloon was the subject of a provisional patent by a civil engineer, William Newton, in 1863. One of his modifications, applicable also to gas-filled balloons, was a parachute round the balloon's waist. The following year, the French aeronaut Eugène Godard built a huge balloon called *L'Aigle*, also a Montgolfier, which made two ascents from Cremorne Gardens, Chelsea. The eagle motif was painted large on the side, and above its waist, about a third of the way from the top, there was a segmented cloth parachute looking like a circular wing or absurdly ill-fitting tutu. In 1874, Albert Fleury came up with a strange variation on the parachute theme. If you attached a weight to the corners of a rectangular plate with cords of equal length, reasoned the inventor, it would drop vertically, but if the cords were unequal it would descend on an incline. The same year Vincent de Groof, a Belgian shoemaker, tried his hand at a flying machine that was a marriage (not, as it turned out, a happy one) between wings and a parachute. De Groof had used his device with poor results in Belgium; now he came to try his luck in London. Before the Cremorne Gardens crowd on 29 June, he fixed his apparatus under the *Czar* balloon, piloted by Mr Simmons. When the balloon rose, the crowd was disappointed to see it swing away into Essex, and the landing that de Groof claimed took place did so well out of sight. There were doubts as to whether he had actually cut free at all, so a few days later he was obliged to repeat the performance so that everyone could see him. This time there were no doubts. 'I must cut you loose,' shouted Simmons. 'Yes,' replied de Groof, 'and I can fall in the churchyard.' Which would have been an appropriate destination. As soon as the rope was cut, the machine collapsed and sent its owner thudding to earth. He died in the Chelsea Infirmary.

A new device, a hybrid parachute-cum-kite, was produced in 1875 by a Joseph Simmons (whether he was de Groof's balloonist or not is unknown). It was designed in fabric strengthened by a net and stretched on a framework, the whole 'parakite' resembling a piece of half-finished abstract paper sculpture. The kite, intended to carry an aeronaut in a car underneath, would be taken up by the wind and then drop like a parachute. The army showed interest, but demonstrations at Chatham the following year proved disappointing; one machine was damaged before or during the flight, and the other crashed – an inauspicious start to the parakite's career that also spelt its finish. But this was to be the fate of the parachute throughout much of the nineteenth century – as no more than a showpiece. Much of the enjoyment must have been offstage, provided by some of the dafter ideas that never took off from the inventor's drawing board.

CHAPTER FOUR

ON WITH the SHOWS

For much of the nineteenth century the parachute underwent little development, its prime function being to add drama to the declining appeal of the simple balloon ascent. It was never considered by balloonists as a means of escape, for it was little use in stormy or windy weather, the sort of conditions in which it might be needed. And there was no room, anyway, in a balloon basket for a stiff-ribbed umbrella-type parachute to be tucked away until required. But James Glaisher, a founder of the (Royal) Aeronautical Society in 1866, thought the parachute might have a future. Writing on aeronautics in the ninth edition of *Encyclopedia Britannica*, published in 1875, he said: 'Though we shall notice any particularly remarkable [balloon] ascents, we shall chiefly for the sake of describing the few that have been undertaken for the sake of advancing science, and which also are of permanent value. It will be necessary to make one exception to the rule, however, in the case of the parachute, the experiments with which require some notice, although they have been put to no useful purpose.'

Ballooning show-business was not, however, itself without scientific value, and in 1880 a new milestone was reached in parachute history. The precursor of the modern parachute was invented – a flexible, unribbed version that would be filled out by the pressure of the air itself. It was not long before cotton gave way to the stronger and less bulky silk, but the parachute of the late nineteenth century was still attached to the balloon or basket by a cord, which had to be cut before descent. The honour for inventing the flexible parachute falls to two men: Thomas Baldwin, an American trapeze artist and tightrope walker (circus performers, as we shall see much later on, play no small part in the history of the parachute), and Capt P. A. Van Tassell, a Dutchman who had settled in America. Although there is doubt concerning the true originator, historians believe the evidence tips the scales slightly in favour of Van

Tassell, though Baldwin has received much of the credit. The new parachute was first tried out in a cattle field outside Los Angeles in the early 1880s. It was dropped from a hot-air balloon in preference to the gas-filled version because the former could be reclaimed when the air cooled, whereas the expensive gas type was often lost. Surrounding Van Tassell were all the show-business trappings that characterised commercial jumps in those days, yet behind the ballyhoo there were undeniable risks: for example, the Dutchman was a heavyweight of 200lb (90.7kg), and the parachute had not even been tested. The canopy itself was unimpressive: it was not shaped, like a modern parachute, but lay on the ground as a large flat disc. The cords from the canopy were tied to a trapeze 15ft (4.5m) below, the whole affair being hung from the balloon's envelope. Van Tassell ascended 4,000ft (1,220m), climbed from the balloon basket on to the trapeze and for a few seconds hung in space. When he cut the parachute's umbilical cord and dropped, the canopy swelled out almost immediately, the shroud-lines tautened, and he touched down safely. Another showman's stunt had been completed, another piece of pioneering accomplished.

The name of Baldwin, Van Tassell's competitor, was remembered when the Dutchman's had been all but forgotten. Possibly the American was better at projecting his extrovert personality. Certainly he made a strong impression on the Prince of Wales (later King Edward VII), for Baldwin was summoned to give a private command parachute-jumping performance before the Royal Family. Baldwin's parachute differed little from that of Van Tassell, from whom, it was alleged, he had purloined the design. If he had, it was a prize piece of ingratitude for the Dutchman had tutored Baldwin with all the parachuting knowledge and expertise he possessed. So the pair went their separate ways, touring much of the world in unfriendly rivalry, each with his own following of young daredevils.

The rewards for parachute jumping could be substantial. One of Baldwin's jumps in the 1880s took place at the Golden Gate Park, San Francisco, where he jumped for a dollar a foot of altitude, thus making 1,000 dollars in a single afternoon. Specialities were developed. A Baldwin pupil, Mark Berg, created a sensation by supporting himself beneath a parachute trapeze with his teeth gripping a leather strap. This stunt proved literally to be his downfall, because one day he bit right through the leather and dropped 4,000ft (1,220m) to his death over Santa Monica,

California. Several other tragedies occurred about this time, one of them involving a double jump – of 'Professor' George Higgins and his wife at a Leeds charity display in 1891. There was a dangerously high wind blowing. Mrs Higgins had just attached herself to the trapeze when her husband joined her. Suddenly, seeing a two-foot tear develop in the balloon's envelope, officials leapt forward and hauled Mrs Higgins clear of the bar. Her husband, unaware of the damage to the balloon, shouted 'Let go!' and in the confusion was whisked away skywards on the crossbar. A gust of wind carried the balloon against some telegraph wires and Higgins was swept off the bar, hurtling down backwards to his death on a barrier below. At another charity show, a twenty-three-year-old woman parachutist, Maud Brooks of Liverpool, was crippled for life during a Whitsun jump in Dublin. She jumped from a balloon but her parachute failed to open until a few feet from the ground. The local paper, the *Freeman's Mail*, commented bitterly: 'We have not conquered the beast in our nature when the element of danger in a parachutist descending from an altitude of 3,000ft [915m] can attract thousands of eager spectators. The evil is aggravated, if anything, when the performer is a woman.'

Several new parachute designs emerged, including a notable one in 1888 by an Italian, Guillermo Antonio Farini, and Baldwin – a flexible mushroom-shaped silk parachute without ribs and with an aperture in the top. The aperture may have been the result of diligent research by Baldwin; on the other hand there is something attractive about the story that the idea came to him from a boy bystander who had been watching a particularly unstable drop by Baldwin in his flexible parachute. 'Mister,' said the boy, 'why don't you put a hole in the top?' What Baldwin had produced was a usable collapsible parachute capable of being carried by a moving aircraft. Not that a moving aircraft was to hand, however: the Wright brothers and sustained powered flight was some fifteen years in the future. Add another fifteen years to that for life-saving parachutes. Thomas Moy, an engineer and patent agent who had invented and built a model steam-driven tandem-wing monoplane and tested it on a circular track at Crystal Palace in 1875, was contemptuous of the Farini–Baldwin parachute and accused them of pandering to the multitudes for money with something that could have been predicted by a schoolboy. 'So far as science is concerned,' wrote Moy in the *Mechanics' Magazine* in 1890, 'they have done literally nothing.' Curiously blind to the possibilities for parachute escape from a heavier-than-air machine such as he himself had been trying to perfect, Moy scoffed at Baldwin's claim that he could manoeuvre his canopy, and urged looking to nature for steerable parachutes, in particular to the squirrel: 'The flying squirrel is a living parachute . . . When he starts from one tree to a lower branch on another, he does not miss his aim. Baldwin could not do that. But then the flying squirrel is not provided with an umbrella-top to do that trick with. He has extended aeroplanes [wings].' Moy said the squirrel would come a cropper if it tried to fall vertically. 'But it is too wise for that; it starts with initial velocity in a horizontal direction and so comes down very gently.' The 'wretched, unscientific gas-bag, and the pretty umbrella cover', added Moy scornfully, were ancient history.

In July 1888, Baldwin and Farini patented the simple limp silk parachute, an improvement on Van Tassell's. Of its steerable quality, he wrote: 'The parachute I can pull down on any side according to the direction I wish to go, I can tilt up the ring one side and pull it down on the other, or I can seize the rope on one side of the parachute and pull the silk down, so as to give it more or less resistance.' On 28 July Baldwin, aged twenty-eight, made his first jump in England in the grounds of Alexandra Palace in London using his improved ribless parachute. Controversy had helped, in the advance publicity, to put Baldwin at the top of the bill above such attractions as 'The Last Days of Pompeii,' a magnificent firework spectacular based on Lord Lytton's book, complete with temples, palace, squares, columns, amphitheatres, and even an erupting Vesuvius. The Baldwin event had been the subject of a call in the House of Lords for the Home Secretary to ban it because of possible danger. This was refused, but the publicity helped to guarantee an attendance of 30,000 spectators, including curious members of both Houses. Baldwin certainly gave his audience value for money – a low-level jump, which carried considerable risk. Sitting on a trapeze he ascended beneath his balloon to about 1,000ft (305m), then threw himself off, freefalling for about four seconds, according to an eyewitness, before deploying his parachute. 'When the parachute was opened, it spread out all at once like an enormous umbrella . . .' wrote the *Daily Telegraph*'s reporter, 'and finally Baldwin reached the earth unhurt in a field outside the Palace grounds.' When Baldwin returned he spoke to the crowd, telling them rather mournfully that for only the second time in his career he had lost his balloon. It seems he had been unable to open the valve and discharge the gas to bring it down. His parachute was described as a 'hood' of fine tussore Indian silk with a system of cords attached, but without a rigid stay or hinge. Experience, he had said, would enable him to judge the angle of descent due to any particular wind, and on that occasion he had come down to within a few feet of the spot aimed for.

But parachute jumps as spectacles were still regarded as unnecessary risks pandering to poor public taste. In that same issue of the *Telegraph*, and on its leader page, the paper addressed the question of display jumps, referring to Baldwin's 'extraordinary exhibition of foolhardiness which almost by a miracle passed off without a fatal result. The odds were many hundreds to one that [he] would be dashed to pieces, as the unfortunate Cocking was more than fifty years ago. Happily, Mr Baldwin escaped a horrible death; but the facts that he has performed the same feat several times before in his own country, and that he has so far saved his own skin, do not detract one iota from the extreme peril which he deliberately underwent. It is absolutely disgraceful, in a civilised country, and in the capital of a great Empire, that the police authorities should allow any man to undertake dare-devil feats, the only purpose of which is to amuse so many thousand curious persons when there is a whole army of chances in favour of the experimentalist having his brains knocked out.' Baldwin's success, said the paper, had proved nothing that had not been proved fifty times before, and when some madcap or mountebank tried to emulate his feat and the parachute collapsed or descended upon houses and the madcap or mountebank died, the Home Secretary would perhaps awaken to the expediency of prohibiting these 'dangerous, demoralising and useless exhibitions'. The paper believed that in real emergencies balloonists would find the balloon envelope would tend to blow up to the top of the netting and form its own parachute.

Indeed, balloonists were always trying to find reliable ways of doing so. Capt William Dale, an Englishman, conceived the idea of a central tube up through the balloon, this housing a cord connected to a layer of oiled silk at the top. Emergency action was to tug the cord and remove the oiled silk to allow the balloon's envelope to surge up the net, but fully under control because the lower valve could rise up the centre tube to the top and keep the 'canopy' stable as it went. But in 1892, four years after Baldwin's jump and the *Telegraph*'s article, Dale was killed when his balloon burst at Crystal Palace without his device to save him.

The same year a French aeronaut, Louis Capazza, invented a 'safety parachute' for a balloon resembling a closely fitting egg cosy. The idea was that if the balloon burst, like Dale's, the gas would be pushed out into the parachute above and through a chimney in the apex. Capazza tested this successfully in Paris at 3,700ft (1,128m) when, using a grapnel, he deliberately and daringly ripped his balloon, *Le Caliban*, from top to bottom. Two months later he brought the balloon to England, but quickly fell foul of the English crowds at a demonstration at the Welsh Harp, Hendon. During preparations for the ascent there was confusion among his assistants, and the parachute 'hat' got twisted awry. In the mêlée the balloon went up, but without the 'parachute', which added to the chaos by fluttering down like a cloak over the struggling ground crew below. 'Give us back our bobs!' came the angry cries from the 6,000 spectators deprived of a show, and after a promise of another performance the following week a crestfallen Monsieur Capazza was hustled into a hansom cab and escorted away by police. But the crowd never did get their bob's worth from a second performance. It was never given, for Capazza was too disgusted at the crowd's behaviour to venture back.

Sometimes primitive airships were designed with some kind of built-in parachute device for emergencies. It might have been nothing more than a canopy fixed above it. In one case the blades of fans, intended to give lift, were designed to flatten and close up to form a kind of parachute. A German, Ludwig Rohrmann, found a new use for the parachute with his parachute-carrying rocket. This was intended for surveying or reconnaissance, the parachute dropping with a camera for taking bird's-eye-view observation shots. In the United States, some inventors saw parachutes as a means of escaping from burning buildings, thus echoing the demonstration jump by the French physician Lenormand in 1783. One innovator, Benjamin B. Oppenheimer of Tennessee, made the naïve claim in 1879 that his 'New and Improved Fire Escape' would enable jumpers to leap from a blazing building of any height and land without injury. Since Mr Oppenheimer's parachute was designed to be only four or five feet (1.2m or 1.5m) in diameter and be harnessed to the wearer's head, not even the padded overshoes thoughtfully provided would have cushioned a fall. To the possibility of death by fire would have been added the certainty of death by parachute.

An early forerunner of the ejection seat also made its appearance in American balloons. A case was divided into two compartments, one containing black powder and the other a parachute jumper. When the required height was reached, the case was thrown out, the parachutist lit the powder, a trapdoor opened and out burst the jumper, parachute billowing amid clouds of smoke. This elaborate attempt to enliven balloon jumping inevitably went wrong. One stunter substituted dynamite for the powder and succeeded in blasting himself to eternity and everything else rapidly to earth. In another case a trapdoor jammed and the parachutist was stifled and burnt to death.

CHAPTER FIVE

DOLLY LEAPS TO FAME

M any women in Victorian and Edwardian times were far from being simpering flowers in whom courage and a sense of adventure might have seemed unladylike. The cavalcade of aeronautical history is sprinkled with women aviators, balloonists and parachutists. There were many in the mould of Jeanne Geneviève Garnerin, whose husband, André-Jacques, in 1797 became the first human being to parachute from a balloon and live. Before her marriage, Jeanne Geneviève became the first woman parachutist, and André-Jacques's niece Elisa made nearly forty jumps as a professional. A rival, Magdeleine Blanchard, came to a tragic end by being burnt to death when her balloon caught fire in an aerial firework display. Later, in the twentieth century, Katchen Paulus, Germany's most famous woman parachute pioneer and performer, had made nearly 150 jumps by the time she retired in 1909. Four years later, Tiny Broadwick, an experienced American jumper, became the first woman to parachute from an aircraft. Another first was scored by pretty twenty-one-year-old Sylva Boyden, who made her thirteenth parachute descent as the only woman jumper in the RAF's first air pageant in 1920. Today, women parachutists compete against each other at a world level, with state-of-the-art parachutes and sophisticated equipment which emphasise the daring of the early parachutists – men and women – who rode the skies with minimal equipment, then threw themselves off the side of the basket of a gas-filled balloon thousands of feet up, as entertainment.

There is no doughtier representative of women's achievements in the past two hundred years than the Edwardian parachutist Dolly Shepherd, who had more than her share of danger and excitement and whom the author had the pleasure of meeting in 1972. Dolly performed before large crowds at venues in many parts of Britain, but her base was the Alexandra Palace, popularly known as 'Ally Pally', in north London. She is remembered there today in a large mural, near the Great Hall, which depicts people and scenes from the Palace's life as a crowd-drawing focus of public entertainment from the time it opened in 1875 and reopened in 1898. Among these, in a familiar pose in natty uniform of peaked cap, knickerbocker suit and high-legged boots is the figure of Dolly Shepherd, the parachute queen who reigned over the skies above the Palace grounds between 1904 and 1912.

Dolly was born in Potters Bar, Middlesex (now Herts), in 1886. Later, her family moved to New Southgate, within sight of the Palace. One day, as a girl of seventeen, she wanted to hear a Palace concert to be given by the American March King, John Philip Sousa. Unable to obtain a ticket, she applied for a job as a waitress in the Great Hall. Here she met the famous Texas showman, Samuel Franklin Cody. It was a fortuitous encounter. On one occasion, during Cody's shooting act in the Bijou Theatre, his wife grazed her scalp, and Dolly offered to stand in for her. This meant posing with a plaster egg on her head while Cody potshotted it blindfold – fortunately successfully. Cody was not only a showman but an aeronautics pioneer, who five years later, on 16 October, 1908, won a place in air history by flying the first heavier-than-air machine in Britain, at Farnborough: his own biplane, called Army Aeroplane Number One, which flew 1,390ft (424m). (Five years later, by now a naturalised British citizen, he died in a plane accident at Aldershot.) Cody's enthusiasm contributed much to Britain's increasing air-mindedness. He certainly aroused Dolly's keen interest in aeronautics, inspiring her when he showed her the experimental work he was carrying out on man-lifting kites at his workshop in Alexandra Palace, and introducing her to Captain Auguste Gaudron, a French impresario of balloon ascents and parachute descents, and a pioneer of lighter-than-air flight.

Gaudron invited Dolly to join his team of parachutists, based at the Palace, tactfully forebearing to mention to Dolly that she would be replacing another woman member of his team who had been seriously injured. Dolly's equipment and method in 1904 would today be regarded as rudimentary, even crude. Her first descent was made sitting on the edge of a balloon basket which contained four passengers, her limp, full-length parachute being attached with string to the balloon netting at a point halfway down its 'waist'. Gripping a wooden trapeze bar with both hands, with only a 'sling' of webbing between her legs to help take the weight of her body, she jumped off the basket at 2,000ft (610m). Her weight broke the retaining string, and she fell straight down for about 300ft (91m), by which time the parachute had fully opened. She floated into a field previously chosen by Captain Gaudron, and as instructed threw herself on to her back to sustain the shock. She told a small gathering of people who had suddenly turned up, of the 'wonderful sensation' of it all. Then she returned in a pony and trap to a heroine's reception at the Palace. For that introduction to aeronautics she was paid £2 10s (£2.50), perhaps worth £90 or £100 today. By the standards of the time this was a substantial fee, but to Dolly the importance lay in the thrill and sense of achievement. In the years that followed, she made dozens more jumps, gaining the confidence that accompanies experience, and the coolness and skill to cope with the unexpected.

Dolly had begun parachuting at a climactic point in aeronautical history. After a century's dreaming and striving to copy the birds, human beings had at last won their wings. On the other side of the Atlantic, the brothers Orville and Wilbur Wright had scored their momentous world 'first' on 16 December 1903, achieving controlled flight in a powered heavier-than-air machine near Kill Devil Hills in North Carolina. But taking to the air was one thing; wrestling with the hazards that accompany flight quite another. The parachute had been in existence for a century, but its lifesaving potential had hardly registered. It was a plaything still and a dangerous one at that, as parachutists such as Dolly Shepherd recognised, despite their apparent insouciance.

On one occasion, in Grantham, Dolly missed landing in front of an express train, thanks to the quick thinking of the driver, who let off steam! Another time, in the Midlands, her parachute had at first refused to open and she made an unscheduled freefall of nearly 5,000ft (1,525m) before it did, at tree level. She landed safely, and was lucky to be only badly shaken and covered with bruises. It was, however, one of her descents, at Longton, a few miles north-west of Uttoxeter (Staffs), in 1908 that brought her to within an ace of tragedy.

Not long before, Captain Gaudron and two others had set up a world long-distance record by completing an event-filled journey from Crystal Palace to Abelar in the Russian province of Novo Alexandrovsk, a distance of 1,150 miles (1,851km). His vehicle was his appropriately named *Mammoth* balloon, the biggest ever made in Britain at that time. Gaudron had brought this balloon with him for the Longton event, and from it Dolly and a young novice jumper, Louie May – a worker at her aunt's Ostrich Feather Emporium in London – were to make a double parachute jump from the basket. However, a short, sharp shower of rain had prevented the *Mammoth* from inflating, and what gas was piped in soon filtered away again. So Dolly's own solo balloon, which she had used earlier for a descent at nearby Ashby-de-la-Zouch and had brought with her, had to serve as a substitute. This meant that Gaudron had to improvise an additional means for Louie to release herself. The balloon was inflated, and he attached two parachutes in position, one on either side of it between the neck and waist. At around eight in the evening, Dolly and Louie stood astride their slings and held tightly to their bars; and the balloon rose, with Dolly waving her Union Jack to the crowd as they were cheered skywards.

It was Louie's first balloon ascent, and she enthused at the silence of space and the intriguing view of the small world below. At around 3,000ft (915m), Dolly suggested it was time to go down, and asked Louie whether she was ready. 'I'll pull away now,' she replied confidently. Dolly made ready to release the rope linking them, about eight feet apart, and Louie tugged at her liberating cord. There was no response. She tried again. And then again. Still no response. The fact was that she was a prisoner, thousands of feet up. In the meantime, the balloon was still rising, now towards a belt of cloud. They were about 8,000ft (2,440m) up, and Dolly was desperately anxious in case Louie might be unable to hang on. She pulled Louie towards her with the connecting cord and made one final attempt to free the mechanism. But it was no use; it was completely jammed. By this time they had entered the cloud belt and at about 11,000ft (3,355m) were wrapped in mist. There was now no point in hoping to try to make individual descents, and Dolly knew there was nothing for it but for both of them to go down on her parachute, and trust it would bear them both. 'You're very plucky!' she shouted to Louie, by way of trying to boost morale, without revealing her concern. She reinforced this by quickly explaining her plan. Louie, in no position to offer an alternative solution, let Dolly talk her through the delicate, dangerous process of transferring from her parachute to the other. It was long, arduous and, thousands of feet up, extremely risky. Any false move by Louie in edging across at the same time discarding her trapeze bar and sling could send her hurtling below. Carefully instructed by Dolly at every stage, Louie slowly transferred her body over to Dolly's. Having wriggled out of the sling, she put her legs round Dolly's waist and her arms round her neck. Then, straining to reach her own ripping cord, Dolly tugged hard, praying that nothing would go wrong. Providence was kind; nothing did go wrong, and both of them fell earthwards on the one parachute. The hope now was that the faster rate of their descent would still let them down safely. As she intended, Dolly landed first, her feet touching down and bearing the entire brunt of the shock, as Louie bounced heavily on her. They came to earth at a roadside near the village of Leigh, about fourteen miles from Longton, where they had first taken off. Louie was able to clamber to her feet, but not so Dolly, who was clearly in trouble. Although she was not conscious of pain, she felt there was something seriously wrong. Farmers and their families suddenly appeared and tried to help her to her feet, but she insisted on lying still, and asked for a doctor.

Dolly's injuries turned out to be serious. Hitting the ground at speed, it turned out, had caused concussion of the pelvis and spinal paralysis, and it would be some time before she could move her legs. She was cared for by Farmer Hollins and his wife and daughters, and although warned she might never walk again, a local doctor gave her a primitive form of 'electrical' treatment, using only a battery and the farmer to complete the circuit. Dolly was made of stern stuff. It was not enough to have survived; she was impatient to be up and about again and to return to the Ally Pally team. Within eight weeks she bravely announced she would soon be parachuting again, as indeed she did.

Today, this near-fatal adventure is enshrined in the *Guinness Book of Records*, and in other books worldwide, as the first mid-air rescue of another parachutist. There is now admiration for such achievements, but at the time killjoy voices were soon raised. One of several critics, the Rev Edmund Pigott, a parish priest, wrote: 'There is nothing in parachute work that justifies the risk that it necessarily entails . . . These and all similar performances . . . only appeal to the lowest instincts of a man's nature, and are in a sense educationally degrading. My own opinion is that all matters such as this need most careful supervision. Parachute descents should be forbidden.'

It was not until after the first edition of my book was published – sixty-five years after Dolly's accident – that I knew she had survived her ordeal. Reading contemporary accounts, mostly from newspapers, I had known nothing more than that she had been injured. It was only after the book's original publication that I heard from her daughter, Molly Sedgwick, who had seen a review, that the story had a happy ending. I had assumed the worst, but here was Dolly's daughter assuring me that her mother was alive and well and living in Eastbourne, and would I like to visit her? I would indeed. It turned out to be a most rewarding experience, and I spent a pleasant hour or two with her as she reminisced, leafing with her through her collection of photograph albums and scrapbooks.

After Dolly's memorable double jump in 1908, she continued her exhibitions, mainly solo, sometimes jumping off a balloon basket, sometimes from a parachute suspended beneath it, or descending solo from a gas or hot-air balloon, either from London venues such as Alexandra Palace, or in exhibitions nationwide. On one occasion at the Palace she had gone to watch a display as a spectator, for a change. The parachutist had failed to turn up, so Dolly offered to take her place, and because she had not come prepared, had to hitch up her long dress between her legs and pin it to her waist in order to make the ascent.

For these parachutists, risk was simply a way of life; you never knew if or when your fate would be dictated by the Almighty or Aeolus. Sometimes a team member would have an accident – as a result of tangled cords or twisted canopy perhaps – and never survive to jump again. Among them was a predecessor of Dolly's, Maud Brooks, whose first parachute descent was in 1897. No fuss was made when a parachutist disappeared; it was philosophically shrugged off and the ranks closed, for fear of demoralising the crowd and deterring local organisers from arranging further parachuting events.

After recovering from the Longton double descent, Dolly returned to her fulltime work at her aunt's Ostrich Feather Emporium in Holborn, where Louie had originally worked. Louie's fiancé, however, who did not approve of parachuting anyway, was extremely angry about the Longton accident, and Louie disappeared from sight. Dolly continued her parachute descents until 1912, when something happened that was to change the direction of her life. In the spring of that year, when she was thousands of feet above Alexandra Palace, and very much at peace with the world, she had a mystical experience.

She described this incident in her autobiography, *When the 'Chute Went Up*:

> The silence of the sky was suddenly broken. It was a voice. I did not imagine it. It spoke once, quite clearly, then no more: 'Don't come up again, or you'll be killed ...' Then with no

emotion and no regret, and for the last time ever, I reached for the ripping cord . . . As soon as I was back at Aunty's house, I rolled up my parachuting costume and put it in the ragbag. Calmly I told my aunt that my parachuting days were over. 'Thank God,' she said. I did.

There were other priorities anyway, for by now, Dolly was twenty-five years old, and World War I was looming. At the outbreak of war she joined the Women's Emergency Corps, then the Women's Volunteer Reserve, while driving munitions for the War Department. When the Women's Auxiliary Army Corps (WAAC, the first of the women's Services) was formed she volunteered to serve in France as a driver mechanic and was attached to the Army Service Corps, driving officers to the Western Front. After the war she married Captain Sedgwick, whom she had driven in France. They lived in south-east London, on the outskirts of Blackheath, and had a daughter, Molly. During the 1930s she carried out voluntary welfare work, being attached to several schools.

Another time, another war . . . In World War II, Dolly became Shelter Staff and Welfare Officer for Lewisham, and afterwards the family moved to the Isle of Wight. Her husband died in 1956, and Dolly and her daughter moved to Eastbourne in 1963, where she met a number of modern parachutists. She died there in 1983, just two months short of her ninety-seventh birthday. Both the Red Devils and the Falcons were represented at her funeral.

During the latter part of her life, Dolly Shepherd had been been delighted to meet some of the dashing parachutists of latter-day, the Red Devils and the Falcons, the daring young men in the display teams of the Parachute Regiment and RAF, and that young luminary of a more sophisticated sport parachuting era, world champion Jackie Smith. How remote their exploits must have seemed for Dolly, who had swung up to the heavens suspended by a sling and with nothing but a wooden bar to hold on to.

Four years after Dolly's death, Molly was able, vicariously, to fulfil an ambition of her mother's – to enjoy the thrill of freefall. Molly performed a tandem jump from 12,000ft (3,660m) in aid of charity and in Dolly's memory, and a film of it was shown in television's *Blue Peter* programme. One of two subsequent jumps she made was with the Red Devils.

Ultimately, Dolly was able to look back from the vantage point of old age and survey a panorama stretching across more than eighty momentous years of aviation history. A fulfilled life indeed.

CHAPTER SIX

TOWARDS HAPPY LANDINGS

From the sandy coast of North Carolina on 17 December 1903, two brothers, Orville and Wilbur Wright, excitedly sent a telegraphed message to their father. It told him that they had become the first men ever to achieve sustained flight with a powered aircraft. For that morning the *Flyer*, their twelve-horsepower, 40ft (12m) wingspan biplane, had made four flights, the shortest of twelve seconds, the longest of fifty-nine.

Man had won his first victory over the skies. But he was not yet master of his fate; he was as strong, or as vulnerable, as the flimsy machine that bore him. So it is strange that although the first parachute jump had been made more than a century before, no serious attempt had been made to adapt it to the demands of a powered plane. The overwhelming preoccupation was with perfecting aircraft capable of remaining in the air, and with improving their performance, rather than a means of escape in an emergency. Neither the Wright brothers nor Blériot, the first man to fly across the Channel, ever carried a parachute for emergency use, nor did any other pioneer of flight up to World War I. In this period, more than 300 pilots the world over lost their lives. Two in every five of these had fallen more than 300ft (91m), which was reckoned a sufficient height for the safe use of a parachute. Thus equipped, they could have survived.

But although their moment had not yet arrived, parachute designers were not idle. In America, as early as 1905, Ralph Carhart laid unofficial claim to using his own freefall-type parachute. The canopy was stored in a chest pack, and a small pilot parachute lay on top of that. It was a primitive affair, but just about practicable. The pack was held closed by safety pins which Carhart had to undo when he dropped into space. The pilot parachute filled out and tugged the larger one from its container. Charlie Broadwick, a balloon jumper bent on providing greater thrills for his public, made a virtue of a piece of parachute trickery. He made his parachute pack as unobtrusive as possible, so that the crowd would see him apparently without a parachute at all. Then suddenly the canopy billowed open, drawn out by a rope 'static line' attached to the balloon by a delicate system of thin thread. He used it hundreds of times and found it far more reliable than established parachutes, which occasionally failed. Another early step towards a fully freefall parachute was taken by A. Leo Stevens, an American, in 1907. He devised a new type whose unique feature was a ripcord, the canopy being jerked out of the pack by whalebone springs. Not for several years was anyone enterprising enough to try it out from an aircraft.

In the meantime, deaths from air accidents were rising so steeply that in April 1910 a Frenchman, Col Lalance, instituted a 5,000-franc prize to be awarded in a competition to the inventor of the parachute which could be dropped with a dead weight of 200kg (441lb) from a height of 600 metres (1,968ft) and show the slowest rate of descent. The response was disappointing, and it was not until the Colonel doubled his prize the following year that inventors began to take notice. One competitor, a Monsieur Bonnet of Grasse, demonstrated his parachute at Saint-Cloud on 16 March 1912 from the balloon *Hélène*. Beneath it was a model of an aircraft fuselage about 20ft (6m) long, and there the parachute was stowed, with a dummy in the cockpit. When Bonnet cut the cable over Charmentray, the parachute opened, the fuselage crashed, but the dummy seated inside landed without a mark.

Fifteen days earlier, the first parachute jump had been made from an aircraft flying at full speed. At this period, loss of equilibrium was considered to be an aircraft's biggest danger, so Thomas Benoist, the owner of an aviation school in Kinloch Park, St Louis, decided to promote a parachute jump from a flying aeroplane, a feat hitherto thought either impossible or crazy. The guinea-pig was 'Captain' Albert Berry, son of a balloonist and himself a professional parachute jumper. Twice the attempt had to be delayed because of bad weather. Then on 1 March the aircraft, a Benoist 'pusher' biplane (so-called because its propellers faced the rear) piloted by Anthony Jannus and carrying Berry, took off from Kinloch and flew 18 miles (29km) to the army post of Jefferson Barracks on the other side of St Louis, where the attempt was to be made. The parachute was carried in a galvanised-iron cone fixed to the undercarriage, its mouth facing the rear of the aircraft until just before the drop. From the mouth emerged two ropes connected to a trapeze bar, which had two leg loops at its ends. The plane, travelling at about 55mph (88.5 kph), soared to 1,500ft (457m). With the drop seconds away, Berry hinged down the metal cone, climbed down through the fuselage frame to the axle and put his legs through the loops. He tied a belt round his waist and then cut himself away, his weight drawing the parachute from the container. It was a perfect drop. 'The experience,' said Berry on landing, 'confirms the feasibility of such descents. I dropped fully 500ft [152m] before the parachute opened, and admit to feeling uneasy. But really, the greatest danger was to the pilot of the plane. I am glad he came out of that successfully.' His reference to the pilot was prompted by a fear that the sudden loss in weight might disturb the aircraft's stability, though Jannus later denied any ill effects whatever. For Benoist himself, pleasure at Berry's successful jump was tarnished with some disappointment: first, because he arrived at Jefferson Barracks just too late to see the jump; second, had the pair taken up an official barograph with them, they would probably have been able to chalk up two American records – for altitude with a passenger and for rapid climbing without a passenger. Berry repeated his jump nine days later, this time in public. It was a bitterly cold day, with strong winds and enough snow to hamper visibility. So that spectators could see the performance, Berry dropped from 800ft (244m), a feature which nearly cost him his life: the parachute got below him at one point and he almost became wrapped in the canopy. Although he reached ground safely, he vowed he would never jump again, unless the financial rewards were more worthwhile.

In France, Monsieur Bonnet, much encouraged by the success of his experiment at Saint-Cloud, announced a new and more ambitious one at Buc airfield, with a human being and from a plane in flight. The jumper was Adolphe Pégoud who would both fly and jump solo. When the police heard of the plan, they tried to ban it, but the mayor intervened and the show went on. Among the spectators was Louis Blériot, whose flight across the Channel back in 1909 won the *Daily Mail's* £1,000 prize. Pégoud took off in his plane at seven in the evening of 19 August 1913, climbed to 750ft (229m), set the controls, put the plane into a dive and allowed the deploying parachute to pull him from the cockpit. Within a few seconds he had made a safe if graceless landing in the top of a tree. Blériot, a keen observer, was as fascinated by the plane's behaviour after Pégoud's exit as he was appreciative of his pupil's jump. For the plane sailed on, embarked on a neat loop-the-loop, then made a perfect landing on its own, suffering only trifling damage. At

Blériot's suggestion, the loop-the-loop (piloted version) became one of Pégoud's regular stunts. He performed it the following month, having been beaten to the global honour of being the first of all time by a Russian, Nesterov, at Kiev on the day of the Buc jump. Pégoud's descent with the Bonnet parachute nevertheless made him the first in Europe to jump from an aircraft; as a result, Bonnet's silk canopy gained considerable prestige, largely because of its speedy and automatic deployment. It was of the 'soaring' type, the canopy billowing out behind and above the aircraft, the pilot being plucked from his seat by the parachute's drag. Also helping the canopy to open were spring-loaded devices and a pneumatic ring round the canopy's circumference which could be inflated with compressed air when the pilot chose.

In 1910 and 1911, Robert Esnault-Pelterie and Gaston Hervieu had tried to adapt parachutes to aircraft. The former devised an anti-shock belt which could be connected to a parachute by elastic bands and was fitted with a ripcord release. It was an exceptionally compact device, weighing a mere 15lb (6.8kg) and folding into a flat parcel over the back of the fuselage. Unlike Bonnet's parachute, with its compressed-air belt, Hervieu's incorporated metal springs. When it was packed in a box, the lid closed and compressed the coils; when opened, the skirts unfolded within a second. Its main disadvantage, however, was its complexity. It received trials at Boulogne in 1910, and underwent tests a year later from the Eiffel Tower before the Ligue Nationale Aérienne with a mock-up aircraft and dummy figure. The parachute, fixed to a collapsible trapeze behind the pilot's seat, spread out at the pull of a lever. No encouragement for parachute experimentation was forthcoming from the aviation press, which seemed remarkably complacent. On 8 October 1910, a *Flight* magazine editorial asserted: 'The idea of providing pilots with parachutes as a possible source of safety in the event of a mid-air calamity does not commend itself to us because, in our opinion, the aeroplane itself is inherently the safest form of parachute that the pilot or his passenger can have, and they had much better trust their lives to it than abandon posts, than rely upon an apparatus that might quite as easily fail them in an emergency.'

But it takes more than mere opinion to shake the confidence of the determined innovator, and experimentation continued apace. It is interesting to see how often inventors during this period relied on artificial aids such as compressed air and springs to inflate parachute canopies. Baldwin and Van Tassell, proponents of the unribbed parachute, realised years before that air flow did the job perfectly well, and proved it. A parachute's failure to open was of course a very real fear. It happened, for example, to a woman parachutist, the wife of balloonist Cayat de Castella, killed in Brussels in July 1914 – a failure that George Prensiel tried to prevent with his compressed-air apparatus, which faintly resembled an ejection seat. Not only would his compressed-air device fully open the parachute at the required moment, but would force it and whatever was attached to it well clear of the aircraft. There were two containers, one storing compressed air, the other containing the parachute and attached to the pilot's seat. When the valve of the first cylinder was opened, compressed air filled the parachute container, shooting it out and the pilot's seat with it.

But despite the increasing ingenuity of serious pioneers, the foolhardy still put in their risk-ridden appearances from time to time. Franz Reichelt, an Austrian tailor, gambled with fate by trying out, after a mere 15ft (4.5m) jump into a heap of straw, a voluminous parachute-cum-overcoat braced with metal stiffeners – his own patent – from the Eiffel Tower on 6 February 1912. Reichelt had assured the authorities that the drop would be only a dummy one. When he reached the first platform of the Tower, he hooked himself instead of the dummy on to the harness and leapt 180ft (55m) to his death when the parachute failed. Efforts to provide means for saving a plane as well as its pilot also continued. Another innovative Frenchman, Monsieur Mayoux, devised a double parachute, one in each of two tubes. In an emergency, the pilot opened a tap to a compressed-air reservoir. The first parachute was thrust out and pulled the pilot with it; the second would open and bring down the plane. Eiffel Tower tests saved a dummy pilot but crashed the model plane, but at least Monsieur Mayoux experimented instead of taking a chance with the real thing. Capt M. Couade, a French engineer, went even further with a single portmanteau device intended to save pilot and plane *together*. The silk parachute was to be placed inside a tube projecting from the rear of the fuselage. A small pilot 'chute was launched into the wind, hauling out the main one, the heaviest part of which was under the pilot. This ambitious idea was probably saved from costly failure by the intervention of World War I.

Throughout the nineteenth century, France had maintained a strong lead in ballooning and parachuting while in Britain Sir George Cayley, the inventive Yorkshireman, worked on the development of the aeroplane. Now France was to be overtaken in her progress with the parachute by the USA and later by Germany. The most promising man-carrying parachute at this time appeared to be Leo Stevens's 'Life Pack', which in its 1912 form, with an independent instead of a rope-attached ripcord (for forgetful jumpers!), was thoroughly tested by Rodman Law, a steeplejack who had jumped with similar products from the Statue of Liberty, bridges and other high buildings. Stevens's parachute pack, weighing only 25lb (11.3kg), was held closed by piano wire strung through the tips of metal cones inserted through eyelets in the flaps, a remarkably similar system to that used today. A sturdy tug on the ring attached to a cord looped over the jumper's shoulder rapidly slid out the piano wire and the flaps, with springy whalebone embedded, flew open and the canopy pulled out. Harry B. Brown, who flew a Wright biplane from which the steeplejack Law had jumped in October 1912, commented: 'In my mind, not as an exhibition stunt, but as a safety factor, it is the greatest move which has yet been made towards the aviator's safety. You can readily see if a machine were to get on fire or break in two how secure the aviator and his passenger would be; [and] by merely rolling off or falling off, descend with perfect safety.'

But Stevens's design was apparently ahead of its time; so was Charlie Broadwick's 'Patent Safety Pack Vest', a knapsack-type pack with harness straps stitched to a close-fitting jacket and worn on the back. Latterly, too, it was operated by a ripcord. Testing the newer version one day, Broadwick came down on it so easily that he took out a packet of cigarettes and casually puffed his way to earth. An adaptation of Broadwick's parachute was to save the life of Mrs Georgia Thompson, years later. She had joined Broadwick's stunt parachute team in 1908 at the age of fifteen, and made her first aircraft jump from leading aviator Glenn Martin's self-built biplane in Los Angeles on 21 June 1913. The following year, on 4 July 1914 at San Diego, Tiny Broadwick, as she was now professionally known (for show-business purposes she was falsely billed as Broadwick's daughter), created another 'first' by jumping from a plane using a manually operated ripcord parachute. The following year this attractive young woman gave a dazzling display before visiting Congressmen and senior US Army officers. As a result they ordered a few of Broadwick's products, but nothing was heard of them again. As far as they were concerned, parachutes were still simply props for circus acts, without serious

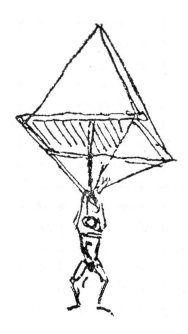

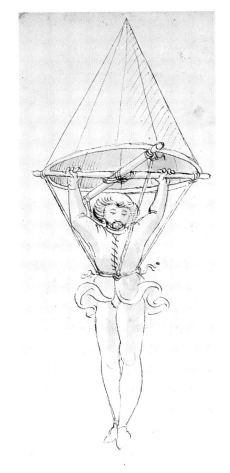

ABOVE: Leonardo da Vinci's sketch of a
pyramid-shaped parachute, *circa* 1485.
(British Museum)

RIGHT: Conical parachute by an unknown
contemporary of Leonardo.
(British Museum)

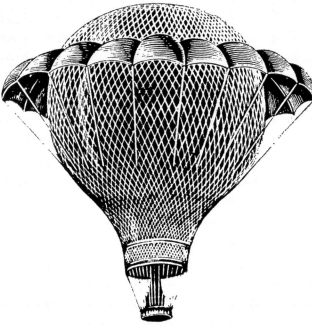

Feranzio's sail-like parachute
'Homo volans', 1595.
(British Museum)

William Newton's balloon with parachute skirt, 1863.

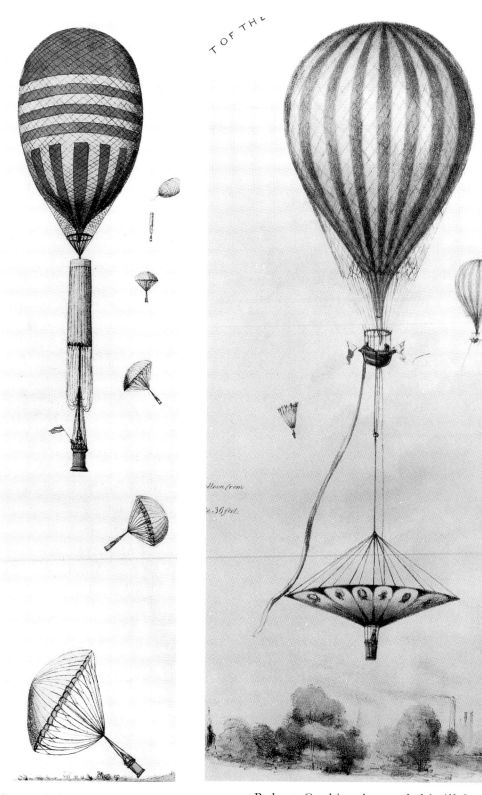

Garnerin's balloon and parachute, showing oscillation, London 1802.

Robert Cocking beneath his ill-fated saucer-shaped parachute, 1837.
(Science Museum)

ixty-one-year-old Robert Cocking, who
arachuted to his death over London,
837.

Robert Cocking's saucer-shaped parachute
eneath the Vauxhall balloon, 1837.

The moment before Franz Reichelt died jumping from the Eiffel Tower with h
parachute overcoat, 1912.

William Newell, sitting on an aeroplane skid before making the first parachute descen
from an aircraft in Britain, at Hendon in May 1914. *(Royal Aeronautical Society)*

eslie Irvin, US ripcord arachute jumper, who anufactured the first scape parachutes for he RAF in the 1920s. *rvin Aerospace)*

ELOW: Major T. Orde-ees, seen on the left, hampioned parachutes or World War I pilots.

The Hon Lt A. E. Bowen, friend of Major Orde-Lees, demonstrates the Guardian Ange
parachute by jumping from Tower Bridge, 1917.

Sylva Boyden, 'the English Air Girl' – made the first first parachute jump by a woman from an aircraft in Britain, 1919.

Dolly Shepherd, the famous Edwardian parachutist, who jumped from balloons over Alexandra Palace, north London.

Inside Everard Calthrop's Guardian Angel parachute factory in London. He had mar champions, but little official support.

Parachutes over Arnhem in 1944 – a picture taken from inside a transport plan
(Imperial War Museum)

purpose. By way of contradiction, though, misfortune led Tiny Broadwick to give a real-life demonstration at an aerial display at the World's Fair at San Francisco in 1915 when the wings of her plane collapsed. Before it crashed, killing the pilot, Tiny had leapt out wearing a Broadwick parachute and was saved. She continued parachuting until 1922, having made an estimated 1,000 jumps.

Hand in hand with the increase in the popularity of flying, deaths from air accidents rose alarmingly during the lead-up to World War I: twenty-nine in 1910, seventy-nine in 1911, 104 in 1912. The statistics disturbed aeronautics experts and flyers alike and the case for parachutes was repeatedly argued. But the stock reply was always handy: that in very few cases would a parachute have helped. Most fatal accidents, it was claimed, occurred too near the ground – while coming in to land – for a parachute to have time to develop. Preoccupation was with the causes of accidents, such as pilot inexperience, faulty construction of the machine (a favourite target for blame), but not remedies. So there were calls for tightening up on construction standards, ensuring the plane's equilibrium, and improvement of the judgement and skill of pilots through proper training. But there was still no provision for emergency escapes. Thus it was possible in 1914 for members of that learned and distinguished body the Royal Aeronautical Society to hear a lecture on 'Lessons Accidents Have Taught' by a Fellow, Col H. C. L. Holden, in which due emphasis was given to the safety belt, helmet, the need for medical examinations, good aircraft design and sound repair work, but without a single reference to the possibility of escape by parachute, either during the main discourse or discussion.

With the approach of war, parachutes, their few far-sighted advocates and their designers ceased to make news, either in Britain or America. In wartime, after all, aircraft were used for fighting, not as jumping-off points for parachute displays. The refusal to recognise the parachute's potential was almost unbelievable. The Royal Flying Corps had been founded in April 1912, and in September the following year, with war in Europe less than a year away, *Flight* magazine was, as ever, sceptical about any role for the parachute: 'Frankly, we see very little future for the parachute as a life-saving apparatus in emergency on aeroplanes; with dirigibles it might be another matter ... Nevertheless, we are far from dissuading the ingenious inventor from persevering with his attempts to devise a really satisfactory folding parachute that can be applied to the body in a moment, and that will open

out with absolute certainty when the person jumps into the air
. . . we fancy that there may be more to be said for the ability to
intentionally leave an aeroplane that is in perfect control than for
the possible virtue of the parachute as a means of checking an
aviator's fall in the event of disaster.' Not much encouragement
there for the aspirant designer.

Yet there were people around with faith to feed the enterprising,
and others who were willing to try to meet the need. One was a
retired railway engineer, Everard Calthrop, the inventor of the
British Guardian Angel parachute who, as we shall see later, found
a cause and lost a fortune. One of the Angel's early champions
was experienced aeronaut and parachutist William Newell, who
on 9 May 1914 used it to become the first Englishman to jump
from an aircraft in flight. Newell, it seems, had few qualms
about the oddly casual way the feat was to be performed. It
took place one evening at Hendon airfield from a five-seater
100-horsepower Graham White aerobus biplane. With the moral
support of another parachutist, Frank Goodden, Newell set about
trying to find a suitable jumping-off point on the plane. Because a
passenger seat was not practicable, he had eventually to settle for
the port chassis skid. Between the front and diagonal skid struts,
a temporary seat was improvised, and on it sat Newell, one foot
in front of the other, a determined and dignified figure with the
40lb (18kg) pack of the Guardian Angel carefully folded and tied
with a breaking cord on his lap. At 7.45 p.m. the aerobus took
off, with Reginald Carr as pilot and Goodden and R. J. Lillywhite
as passengers. It climbed for eighteen minutes to 2,000ft (610m),
then Newell, assisted by a friendly kick from Goodden, jumped
off. Almost immediately, the 26ft (8m) flying diameter parachute
filled out and, after some swing, steadied and brought Newell
down in under two and a half minutes to handshakes and three
cheers from a small crowd. Newell said afterwards that he did
not remember Goodden's 'kick', that in fact he was so cold that
he could not tell whether he was standing on the skid or not!
Somebody announced that any future demonstrations would be
made using a special seat. In recognition of his exploit, the London
Aeronautical Club awarded Newell a well-deserved silver medal.
But appreciated as his jump was by the aeronautical cognoscenti,
Newell's praises were not sung by the public at large, and in the
national newspapers the event rated only a few paragraphs.

CHAPTER SEVEN

ORDEAL BY FIRE

The virtual indifference which greeted Newell's jump at Hendon in May 1914, the first parachute drop from an aircraft in Britain, was to be reflected in a lack of concern for pilot safety throughout World War I on the Allies' side – to the lasting shame of officials and senior staff officers. Parachutes *were* used, but only by front-line kite balloon observers, who were highly vulnerable as sitting targets for enemy air attacks. The parachute was the Spencer attached type, fixed to the balloon basket and jerked from its bag by the jumper's weight.

Admittedly, and strange to say, not all Allied pilots wanted parachutes. Many regarded them with contempt, as if carrying one was in some way an admission of weakness or even cowardice. But even the many who looked upon parachutes as a sensible precaution were prevented by the air authorities from using them. There was simply not the will to push ahead and produce the right type. Why? There were two reasons. First, it was widely and insensitively thought that pilots with parachutes might abandon their aircraft too easily. As *Flight* magazine commented in 1913, 'A pilot's job is to stick to his aeroplane' – even, it seems, unto death. Secondly, because parachutes fell some way short of perfection in design and adaptability, they were considered unsuitable for aircraft use. Thus half a chance of survival took second place to no chance at all. Parachutes had existed in the United States for some years, yet even Broadwick's 'Patent Safety Pack Vest' and Leo Stevens's trusty 'Life Pack' had vanished into obscurity there, and US pilots too were banned from using them. But the Broadwick and the Stevens had been widely publicised in America in the pages of specialist journals, which makes official apathy on both sides of the Atlantic all the more extraordinary. Lack of interest in Stevens's ripcord parachute eventually drove him to make only attached-type parachutes for balloonists.

With drive and encouragement from those in positions of

power, parachutes could undoubtedly have been provided for all who needed them. Instead, there was a deplorable lack of faith in expertise or in pilots' loyalty or intelligence – pilots of the calibre of Sholto Douglas, who went on to become Marshal of the RAF, Lord Douglas of Kirtleside. Amazingly, Lord Douglas did not discover the official attitude to parachutes until shortly before the publication of his autobiography, *Years of Command,* in 1963. His indignation flared after half a century: 'When I . . . thought about what we had to endure and I recalled how so many men had died in such agony, all because somebody had thought so little of us that they believed that providing us with parachutes would encourage us to abandon our aircraft, my anger was roused in a way that is unusual for me.' The fear that was constantly with the front-line pilot was that of fire in the air, Lord Douglas recalled. One of the worst of any airman's experiences was to have to witness the helplessness of a friend going down in flames: 'On one patrol early in 1917 I was flying in formation with my squadron when we were suddenly attacked by some Huns. After the first flurry was over I glanced across at the next aircraft beside me in our formation, and I saw that the observer, poor devil, was standing up in the back seat agitatedly trying to call the attention of his pilot to a glint of flame that was just starting to appear along the side of their aircraft. A moment later there was a violent explosion and the whole aircraft disintegrated. Such a sight was all too common in our flying of those days, and so far as I was concerned it was one of the most horrible that one could witness.'

To observers in the tethered balloons sent up at the front to track enemy troop movements or direct artillery fire, parachutes were salvation indeed. During the war 800 of them, including seventy-six Americans, came to owe their lives to the flimsy sheet of silk, the British version of which was the attached-type Spencer, packed in a characteristic 'candle-snuffer' container slung on the side of the basket. Even then there were scores of casualties, among them the famous contemporary music hall comedian Basil ('Gilbert the Filbert') Hallam, who made a fatal error during an enemy air attack. Hallam jumped to his death believing that he was still tied to his parachute, which had actually become detached.

Balloons were all too easy targets. German fighters swept in and strafed them with tracer and sent them blazing to earth. Retaliation with rifle fire, at first a routine gesture, was soon abandoned because it delayed escape, often crucially. And if the jumper failed to get clear quickly enough, the balloon's flaming bag was likely to drop straight on to him. Officers training for balloon work could volunteer for a practice drop from a captive balloon if they wished, and many did so. But one balloon officer, Stephen Wilkinson, wrote in his book *Lighter Than Air* after the war: 'It required no small amount of nerve to make the effort, and when the actual moment arrived and the jumper looked down to earth about 2,000ft [710m] below there were many cases of "wind up", and we used to put the final touch on by a sudden shove off the side of the basket. The effect of a jump on the remaining occupant left in the basket was rather alarming.'

Sitting targets as they were, these balloonists often displayed admirable coolness and gallantry. In August 1916, a balloon observer, 2nd Lt A. G. D. Gavin, was awarded the DSO for 'conspicuous presence of mind and unselfish courage' in the use of a parachute. When his balloon broke loose and headed quickly for the enemy lines, Gavin explained to his passenger how to use the parachute and helped him out of the basket. Then he destroyed all his papers and came down on his parachute, landing in a hail of enemy gunfire. Both survived. But for the parachute's presence, casualties among balloon observers would have been enormous. Something of the grimness of the ordeal is captured in this German account from *The German Air Force in the Great War*, by G. P. Neumann:

> [The balloon observer] must never allow himself to be disturbed by the thought that, if his balloon were set on fire above him, he would have a few seconds only in which to make his leap for safety with his parachute. As he was unable to see and form any judgement, he had to rely on the officer on ground duty to give him the order to jump. When this order came through the telephone, he had to jump from his basket into the depths below without a second's hesitation.
>
> Even then his troubles were not over. The attacking aeroplane would direct a furious fire against the defenceless man hanging from the parachute and blazing tracer bullets would leap at him. Only extraordinary will-power, self-control, strong nerves and a stout heart enabled him to stand the strain and to go up again after his descent! Many an infantry officer who had applied for training as a balloon observer in order to have a rest from the hardships of the trenches has said, after an experience of this kind, 'I would sooner undergo five days' bombardment than make another ascent.'

Much was now to be heard of a parachute named the Guardian Angel, invented by a former railway engineer, Everard Calthrop. Forceful and often tactless, Calthrop was to be a thorn in Whitehall's side for years to come. Calthrop was pursuing a creditable career before he began making parachutes. He was apprenticed on the railways in England, and in 1882 went out to India. Then in 1910 came a tragedy which changed the course of his life. His great motoring friend the Honourable Charles Rolls (of Rolls-Royce) was flying a Wright biplane in a competition at Bournemouth when the rudder gear snapped and he crashed. To Rolls went the unhappy distinction of being the first Englishman to die in an aircraft accident. Although Rolls was flying too low for a parachute to have saved him, the incident, coupled with the narrow flying escapes of Calthrop's own eldest son, impressed on him the need for a good life-saver. He decided to devote the rest of his life to improving parachutes.

After several years' research came the Guardian Angel. It was given its first official trial by the Admiralty Air Department at Farnborough two months after war broke out, and was warmly praised for its 'automatic' opening system. But its weight of 90lb (41kg) was a big obstacle. Drastic modifications resulted in the A-type, weighing only 24lb (10.8kg), and its length of drop before opening was a mere 80 to 100ft (24 to 30.5m). Calthrop's parachute had one overwhelming advantage on other types: 'positive opening'. A disc, or in later models a wooden ring, about two feet in diameter braced the mouth of the parachute so that when hauled from its cone-shaped container by the weight of the falling pilot, air would pour in and deploy it immediately, and without shock. It was the maker's proud claim that the Guardian Angel, properly used, would never fail. But it had drawbacks. It was vulnerable to enemy fire, because it was stored either under a plane's cockpit or behind the undercarriage. It was also complex, so much so that its meticulously procedured packing would take a skilled man up to two hours.

Tests with the parachute in March 1915 were sufficiently encouraging for Lt-Col Sir Bryan Leighton to drop with it 'live' at low levels. It still failed to be approved for general issue to airmen, but this did not discourage Calthrop. Convinced that orders would soon flood in, he opened a factory in the Edgware Road and formed a private company. Using the combined resources of himself and friends, he had by this time spent an unprofitable £12,000 on research and development. In December 1916 Royal Flying Corps HQ in

France was told that the Guardian Angel parachute had been tested by the Admiralty from BE2c planes, and in every case the parachute opened when it had fallen about 100ft (30.5m). Its superiority and reliability over other types were acknowledged because not only did it open with minimal shock, but air pressure would build up inside directly the parachute was released, giving it a greater tendency to open. In addition, the inventor claimed to have overcome an inclination for the parachute to spin (caused by the ropes unwinding and rewinding as the airman descended). 'No airman,' it was stated, 'has yet made a descent from an aeroplane in one of the parachutes, but several descents have been made from balloons and airships. The inventor claims that they would be most useful for secret service work, and descent at night in the event of a forced landing, as the airman alights so gently.' The following month, trials were carried out at Orfordness Experimental Station, Suffolk with the object of dropping secret agents, and some weeks later up to thirty of them, with black canopies and rigging lines to avoid being picked out by searchlights, were dropped behind the German lines in France. Later they were used for the same purpose on the Italo-Austrian front. In his book *In the Sideshows*, Capt W. Wedgwood Benn described one of these missions, in which he served as navigator and organiser. The intention was to parachute an Italian agent well behind the Austrians. He would then work his way to his native town, gathering information as he went to send back by signal or by one of the carrier pigeons accompanying him. The plane, an old SP-4, carried Lt-Col W. G. Barker VC as pilot, Capt Benn as navigator and an Italian named Alessandro Tandura. Fitted with his parachute, Tandura squatted over a trapdoor through which he would disappear on his mission. The aircraft carried three bombs: two to be dropped on the return journey to disguise the expedition's true purpose, and a third to mislead the enemy in the event of capture. The mission was an outstanding success. Tandura disappeared, clad in military uniform, and when he reached ground he changed into peasant clothing and for three months sent valuable information back to Italian Command. Eventually he earned the Gold Medal for Valour, the Italian Army's highest award.

The value of parachutes for dropping supplies was exploited in 1918 when ammunition was dropped to front-line troops at the battle of Hamel, the starting point for the offensive that led to Germany's ultimate defeat. The inventor was a young Captain, twenty-two-year-old Lawrence Wackett of No 3 Squadron, AFC.

Wackett, who was knighted in 1954, had already gained a reputation as an innovator and had been urged by General Sir John Monash to devise a way of supplying forward troops with ammunition by parachute as a way of reducing casualties. Capt Wackett, who described the process in his autobiography *Aircraft Pioneer*, gave a successful demonstration of his parachute's feasibility by dropping two large cases of ammunition close beside General Monash and the army commander, Sir Henry Rawlinson, from a height of 500ft (152m). As a result, some twenty planes were equipped for ammunition dropping using parachutes 12ft (3.6m) in diameter and wooden ammunition boxes weighing 40lb (18kg) each. The success of the operation earned Wackett Sir John's personal congratulations, but also £300 for his innovations used in the battle, a valuable precursor of supply dropping widely used in World War II. Wackett's fast work on developing equipment in 1918 alas came too late for the attempts made to relieve General Townshend's troops in Mesopotamia under siege in Kut-el-Mara in 1916. The call here was for at least 5,000lb (2,267kg) of supplies every day to feed 12,000 starving troops. The method of conveying them was the crude one of dropping canisters bodily, without parachutes, from low-flying aircraft straight on to the ground. For two weeks until the force surrendered, nine aircraft, escorted by five others, shuttled seven tons of food, along with letters, wireless batteries and medical supplies, much of it wasted because the containers burst open on impact.

Nearer home, the prospect of saving the lives of airmen in action was still as far away as ever. Among members of the Air Board, which had dragged its feet ever since the idea was first mooted, there was little enthusiasm and even hostility. Even supposedly informed opinion displayed an alarming naïvety. Totally ignoring the very real dangers of fire, particularly in fighting machines, Borlase Matthews wrote in the 1916 edition of the *Aviation Pocket Book*: '. . . The many suggestions as to the uses of parachutes in aeroplanes do not take account of the fact that in the case of an engine stoppage or the like, the aeroplane itself acts as efficiently as a parachute and has the additional advantage of allowing the landing ground to be chosen.' In the 1917 edition, the subject of parachutes was ignored altogether.

In August 1917, an unconfirmed report filtered through that a German airman had baled out by parachute and survived. This was seen cautiously by one journal as 'a case for inquiry and, within limits, experiment, but we should scarcely like to go as far as to say that instructions in the use of the parachute should as yet form part of the ordinary course of training of aviators.' And this was in what was to be a year of disaster for young pilots under training. According to a subsequent report to Parliament no fewer than 800 fatal accidents occurred among flying trainees in 1917, and the public were expected to believe Major John Baird, Parliamentary member of the Air Board, when he told the Commons in March 1918: 'No case is known of any officer under instruction providing or wishing to provide himself with a parachute. Experiments are proceeding, but no parachute suitable for use from an aeroplane has yet been arrived at.' This can hardly be reconciled with Everard Calthrop's later disclosure that over a two-year period many officers had applied direct to his company to buy his Guardian Angel parachute, and that 'we informed the Air Board of this and applied for permission to supply them, but sanction was refused'. Capt R. M. Groves, in a minute to the Air Board, reported: 'The heavier-than-air people all say that they flatly decline to regard the parachute in an aeroplane as a life-saving device worth carrying in its present form.' He failed to say which heavier-than-air people were consulted; no doubt these were staff officers deskbound in Whitehall safely distant from the pilots who every day were blazing down like meteors over enemy lines in France.

To be fair, there were admirable exceptions to brass-hat distrust of the parachute, notably Major T. Orde-Lees, future Secretary of the Air Board's Parachute Committee. Orde-Lees was a restless eccentric passionately dedicated to the parachute campaign. The trouble was he also attracted considerable unpopularity among his colleagues. Not that unpopularity bothered him, or that it was a novel experience. He was disliked for his exhibitionism at school, unpopular as a young Royal Marines officer, and when in 1914 he went out with Shackleton's Imperial Trans-Antarctic Expedition, his talent for alienating himself accompanied him there too. When their ship, the *Endurance*, broke up and had to be abandoned, Shackleton left twenty-two members of the expedition on an island to await his return with assistance. It was three months before he could do so, by which time the stranded explorers were in danger of resorting to cannibalism. The question was who would be sacrificed first. To Frank Wild, leader of the stranded group, one name shone out above all others. First choice, unbeknown to him until later, was Orde-Lees.

Fortunately for him, rescue arrived in time, and he survived to carry out his work promoting the parachute cause with great diligence. On Sunday, 11 November 1917, he and Lieutenant the Honourable A. E. Bowen, lately of the RFC, gave demonstration jumps with the Guardian Angel parachute from Tower Bridge into the Thames 150ft (45m) below, watched by the designer and manufacturer, Calthrop. The purpose was to demonstrate, publicly and beyond doubt, that the parachute could open as low as 200ft (61m), and that Calthrop's quick-release device for detaching the harness would work as well in water as on land. Continual delays before the start put Orde-Lees in an impatient mood. He threatened withdrawal, then agreed to continue, but only if he made a head-first dive; feet-first drops reminded him of steep aircraft descents, which he disliked. The Guardian Angel, neatly packed in its muffin-shaped bag, hung from a beam sticking out six feet from the bridge's upper parapet. Orde-Lees wrapped the attaching rope round his right leg and, at a flag-wave from Calthrop, dived down, jerking and somersaulting until the parachute opened. Bowen followed, but feet first in the traditional way. Both jumpers vanished beneath the water, surfaced immediately thanks to their lifebelts, and as the current and breeze carried them downstream they operated their quick-release devices, detached their parachutes and were picked up by a Thames waterman. Thus was performed the lowest-ever human parachute drop to date, several hundred feet lower than the previous one – an answer, it might be thought, to those critics who doubted the parachute's effectiveness near the ground. The demonstration would also have caught the eye of a public which until then might not even have been aware of a parachute's existence.

The war dragged on. In April 1918 the RFC became the RAF. Two months later, Mr Philip Morrell, Liberal MP for Burnley, tried, as he had done before, to persuade the Air Ministry to supply trainee pilots with parachutes 'if necessary at their own expense and allow them to undergo a course of parachuting during their flying course'. Major Baird, Parliamentary member of the Air Board, stonewalled again. He refused to accept Mr Morrell's figure of 800 fatalities among flying trainees the previous year, taking refuge in a 'much smaller' but unspecified total. As for Mr Morrell's suggestions, 'Experiments have been and are still being made, but the great majority of accidents occurred under circumstances which precluded the hope that a parachute would be of any value.' Because of what Calthrop called impatiently 'the general indifference and passive resistance of the authorities', it was not until June 1918 that the Air Board set up a Parachute Committee. General E. M. Maitland, who had made a parachute jump from the airship *Delta*, was appointed chairman, with Major Orde-Lees as secretary. The following month Orde-Lees went to France to report on the Spencer-type parachutes used by the kite balloon observers. These were different from the Guardian Angel, attached type but not 'positive opening', i.e. they had no disc or ring bracing the mouth of the parachute so that air would sweep in and speed up deployment. About one in 200 failed to open. The Spencer harness was unpopular and rarely used because it was not adjustable and became hot and uncomfortable in summer. So each man made his own substitute harness, crude affairs of rope, which they knifed through to free themselves on landing. Some roughly-made harnesses even had parts held together with trouser buttons. The observers had never heard of the Guardian Angel, seemingly a safer design, and nothing would make them try it out. 'They were sceptical of the devil they don't know and prefer the devil they do,' reported Orde-Lees.

There was certainly approval of the Spencer. In 1973, Dr G. S. Sansom of Godalming (Surrey), who served in World War I, wrote to me: 'I had great trust in the Spencer parachute, though I felt nervous before my practice drop. I only had three compulsory drops – when the balloon was attacked – and I enjoyed those. We had no harness supplied at first, so I made a double bowline rope sling, which I always used, though our riggers made nice webbing slings for the other observers.' Calthrop's parachute, on the other hand, had been much more carefully thought through. It was an ingenious piece of craftsmanship, and way ahead of anything so far produced in Britain, and packed so that nothing was left to chance. When pulled out by the weight of the pilot, first came the rigging tapes, carefully folded so that entanglement was impossible. The canopy, which followed it, was so pleated and folded that the longest time taken to deploy after the jump was made was two and a half seconds. There was even a shock absorber to cushion the strain on the jumper's body when the parachute opened. Experiments had proved that installing a parachute on an aircraft might reduce its rate of climb and speed by two or three miles an hour. Orde-Lees added dismissively: 'There is no doubt that the majority of aeroplane pilots desire parachutes irrespective of prejudice to the performance of the machine.' His view was endorsed by Brig-Gen Charles Longcroft, who remarked in France that as far as he and his pilots were concerned, he 'strongly desired that some steps should be taken to obtain and test parachutes suitable for aeroplanes'. He said he had heard the objection that pilots might jump prematurely, but as a practical parachutist himself he did not believe it. Orde-Lees was delighted, and he told Longcroft later: 'It is very encouraging to find that a senior officer who is both a pilot and parachutist has given this matter so much consideration.' Subsequently, Longcroft took command of the RAF division for training pilots, which suffered enormous casualties in air accidents.

Further impetus to the parachute cause was brought about by the death in an air crash in France on 9 July 1918 of one of Britain's leading aces, a newly promoted squadron commander, Major James McCudden VC. McCudden, with a recorded bag of fifty-seven German aircraft destroyed or shot down out of control, was a firm supporter of parachute provision on all aircraft, home-based in France. He was flying one day in an SE5a to take over his new command when he landed at Auxi-le-Château and sought directions from No 8 Squadron headquarters. He climbed back into his plane and took off, but at 700ft (213m) his engine choked and he turned as if to land again. Suddenly he dived into the trees behind the hangars, crashed and was fatally wounded. 'What went wrong may never be known,' one witness said, 'but one wonders whether, if he knew his machine was out of control, he might have been saved by parachute.' There was nothing to save the life either of the daring and much decorated American ace Major Raoul Lufbery. On 19 May 1918 he attacked a German triplane over Toul in France in his Nieuport at 2,500ft (762m), then withdrew when his machine-gun jammed. Sweeping in to renew the attack, the Nieuport suddenly burst into flames, and Lufbery was seen to jump out and hit the ground a quarter of a mile from where his plane crashed.

The establishment of a British Parachute Committee so late in the war, coupled with attempts to fit the parachutes on aircraft simply not built for them, seemed futile. And here at hand was a company of Lloyd's underwriters offering a twenty per cent cut in insurance premiums for pilots, provided they confined their flying to planes equipped with the Guardian Angel. The attitude of the aviation press was now swinging in favour of parachutes. Following McCudden's death, *Aeroplane* magazine observed: 'One believes firmly that the parachute is as necessary a fitting to an aeroplane as a lifebuoy on a ship, and that it has just as good, or just as slight, a chance of saving lives, according to the circumstances. It is not an infallible life preserver, but it is an excellent insurance policy. That fact should make it worthwhile.' Moreover, *Flight* magazine, which had been sceptical about parachutes since well before the war, now performed a U-turn: 'The fact that a perusal of the, unfortunately, only too frequent accidents to aviators would indicate that a very great percentage of these pilots might have been saved had they been equipped with a reliable parachute is a very strong point in favour of the more general adoption of this useful accessory. We do not doubt that there are a good many people who shrug their shoulders at the idea of a parachute on board an aeroplane. We were inclined to do the same – until we saw Mr Calthrop's parachute.' The dangers of air accidents were eloquently stated when the plane flown by Major Bannatyne caught fire at 1,000ft (305m) after engine failure near Cirencester. To escape the flames creeping along the fuselage, he climbed out of the cockpit and crawled along to the tail, from which he hung by his hands till the flames reached him again. Just before the machine crashed, he dropped clear, surviving with only a broken arm and cuts.

Fire was an enemy to both sides in the air war. Without a parachute, all aircrew could do was to put the plane into a sideslip – as many did – and hope the force of the wind would stifle the fire. 'Sometimes it worked, and sometimes not,' said 2nd Lt Leslie Pargeter, who was transferred from the infantry to the RFC late in the war. Pargeter, who flew as an observer in two-seater RE8 biplanes with Army Cooperation, told me of two missions in the summer of 1918 during which the petrol tank of his plane was damaged by enemy fire. On one observation sortie, the RE8 dropped several bombs on the German lines, then returned to its scheduled task. 'There was a lot of "Archie" [anti-aircraft fire] about,' recalled Pargeter, aged eighty, 'and suddenly, when we were at about 6,000ft [1,830m] there came a loud crack. The petrol tank had been hit by a shell fragment and there was petrol everywhere. The pilot and I were drenched in it. Immediately, of course, one thought of the possibility of fire. So I hopped out on to the lower wing and stuffed my glove into the hole in the tank, which is forward of the pilot. Then we set off for home and landed without trouble.' Three weeks later, they spotted a group of Germans on the ground and swung into the attack, the pilot firing his Vickers as the RE8 dived, Pargeter with the swivelling Lewis from the rear as the plane zoomed across. The Germans promptly retaliated. 'Soon the petrol tank had caught it again

– we were as full of machine-gun bullet holes as a leaky old watering can,' said Pargeter. 'I dropped over the side on to the wing once again and plugged the holes with as many fingers as I could. Luckily, we touched down before running out of petrol.'

Fortunately for them, too, there was no fire. But there was a medal. Pargeter and his pilot earned a General's congratulations for helping to restore contact between infantry units that had lost touch with each other, and Pargeter himself received the DFC for his exploits. He modestly refused to quote the citation to me, but I discovered it had described him as a 'very gallant officer'. 'In these planes,' added Pargeter, 'fire was our third passenger. If we'd caught fire and had parachutes, we'd have used them. But of course we never had them.' In fact, his only experience of parachutes was in carrying out experiments for dropping supplies to forward troops. Pargeter remembers trying, with little success, to drop boxes of parachute-borne ammunition in August 1918 from beneath the engine nacelle of an RE8. 'We didn't know the first thing about parachutes,' he said. 'In one case, when I pulled the release lever the parachute didn't open and the box just shot down through the roof of a hangar, damaging the wings of two aircraft. Then we circled around the base and dropped the other, and the parachute opened beautifully. The trouble was, after I had released it I noticed the padre below, having a nice afternoon bath behind his hut. For a horrible moment I thought it was going to hit him. It missed, but fell on to the roof behind him, and his hut immediately collapsed!'

CHAPTER EIGHT

BIRTH OF FREEFALL

In the summer of 1918 the British Air Ministry received a severe jolt when reports confirmed rumours that had been circulating for some weeks, that the Germans had been making emergency parachute jumps from their planes over the Western Front. Among those who escaped was Ernst Udet, a fighter ace with a score of more than sixty kills to his credit. He was flying over Villers in June when he took on a Bréguet carrying out artillery observation. As the crippled French plane went into a dive Udet chased it down, only to receive a farewell burst at point-blank range from the doomed French gunner. His own petrol tank now smashed, Udet dropped over the side on his parachute, touched down in no-man's-land with a twisted ankle, then crawled 200 yards (183m) to the safety of the German lines. After the war, Udet told a Flying Corps officer, Lt-Col L. A. Strange DSO MC DFC, that he was one of the few who wore a parachute during the war, adding that it had saved his life twice.

An American air force pursuit group shot down eleven German planes, all the pilots of which saved their lives with parachutes. One parachute captured by the Allies was found to be stuffed into a sack ten inches thick, on which the pilot sat. It was designed by Otto Heinecke, and a static line was used to deploy the canopy. Attached to this was a breaker-cord which snapped with the pilot's weight as he dropped. Heinecke had improved on the Guardian Angel with a backpack-type parachute hauled out by a cord attached to the plane. The first were of Japanese silk, and later ones used cruder forms of calico. These may not have been ideal, but they saved lives; that was what mattered. And it is that practicality that distinguished the attitudes towards parachutes between the Germans and the feet-dragging Allies. The news of parachute use by the Germans represented no mean moral victory over the Allies, leading to speculation among our pilots about why *they* were not equipped with them too. So testing was speeded up: in England the

Guardian Angel and Mears, in America the silk and cotton versions of their AEF. France had the Robert, packed into a clumsy bundle with a lanyard projecting from the centre like an apple stalk, the whole strapped to a three-ply board on the pilot's back. All had static lines.

Parachute campaigners in Britain were fired with fresh enthusiasm. Brig-Gen Robert Brooke-Popham, in charge of supplies in France, demanded news of progress in London, seeking suggestions from unit commanders in the field as to how parachutes could be fixed to fighters. The ideas multiplied: under the wings, on the side of the fuselage, in an enlarged locker behind the pilot's seat, on the fuselage behind the pilot's shoulders. 'It would be easier to give more definite suggestions,' wrote the commander of one aeroplane supply depot sardonically, 'if I actually *had* a parachute.' The Allies allowed themselves to be bogged down with problems in the search for perfection, but the Germans had simply taken a chance and jumped. The English put much thought and effort into ways of fitting parachutes on to aircraft, and at Farnborough they succeeded with the SE5, Sopwith Snipe, Bristol Fighter and DH 9; the Camel, however, proved difficult because there was no space in the cockpit, and the fuselage behind the petrol tanks was unsafe because of fire risk. On 23 September 1918, a group which included Winston Churchill, then Minister of Munitions, watched parachute trials with the Bristol Fighter. In one case the parachute caught on the tail-skid. The process of fitting and testing with dummy drops on individual types of aircraft with consequent delays, reports, second thoughts, re-testing and reports back, would clearly take months, if not years. Nevertheless, by September an order for 500 Guardian Angels, duly modified, had been placed with Calthrop. All single-seater fighters, ordered Brooke-Popham, would be fitted with parachutes in France.

Test drops were now made comparing the Guardian Angel and the Mears, a cheaper parachute which was rolled up in a pack on the pilot's back, a cord being attached from the pack to the plane's body. The simple pack was intended to cope with the problem of dropping out of the plane at speed; also, it could be rolled into various widths to suit the dimensions of different types of cockpit. Five hundred of these were ordered. With the help of an RAF officer and a young engineer, Calthrop set about improving release equipment. A pilot parachute and a main parachute were separately housed in compartments in the fuselage. The compartment containing the pilot 'chute could be opened to the airstream, and when the canopy deployed, it hauled out the main. In October 1918, Sir William Bull, Conservative MP for Hammersmith, finally drew a public admission from the government that parachutes were effective as an aircraft safety device. In the Commons he asked the Under-Secretary of State to the Air Ministry 'whether any report has been received as to the use of parachutes by German airmen as a means of escape from injured aeroplanes; and whether the tenor of the report, if any, indicates that the appliance is effective in life-saving'. Major Baird: 'The reply to both parts of the question is in the affirmative.' Two days later the German aeronautical journal *Flug Sport*, noting the immense prejudice against parachutes in Britain, published a detailed illustrated article on the Guardian Angel.

The parachute section of the Air Force Technical Department in Britain was now receiving sufficient misguided ideas for parachutes to have to publish a notice giving guidance to inventors. This emphasised that, given the fulfilment of basic requirements of size – 28ft (8.5m) flat diameter – weight (under 40lb, 18kg, including harness) and rapid production, choice would be governed mainly by considerations of morale. Parachutes depending on an explosive charge, springs or compressed air for their release and deployment were ruled out because they could too easily fail. 'This preys on an aviator's mind, and although "half a parachute" is better than no parachute he will only feel justified in taking greater flying liberties when he knows that the action of his parachute is independent of the function of such devices. In short, the simpler the parachute the better.' Inventors were admonished for ignoring the psychological side of parachutes, which must above all provide the pilot with confidence. Yet inventors 'seem to regard aviators much in the same way as we regard animals used for experimental purposes – as being without cognizance of the dangers to which they are to be subjected.'

All this discussion, albeit prompted by the noblest motives, came a trifle late for the war pilots. By now, thousands of their burned and broken bodies were lying buried under alien skies, men for whom, to borrow the Technical Department's phrase, 'half a parachute' would certainly have been an improvement on no parachute at all. So Armistice Day on 11 November came and went, the cheering and the shouting died, and aircraft as well as swords began to be beaten into ploughshares. The Guardian Angel and the Mears gathered cobwebs, and Major Orde-Lees would arrive home to weep in despair at his Whitehall colleagues' intransigence.

Experimentation continued, but shamefully so did the opposition. Yet almost daily the need for parachutes was stressed by
reports of deaths on training flights. In January 1919, Orde-Lees
saw a young officer, Lt Christopher Berkeley, killed while giving
instruction at Northolt (Middlesex). He was the only regular pilot
who had ever made a parachute jump from an aircraft. 'It is
therefore especially tragic,' wrote Orde-Lees, 'that he should have
met his death in an accident where a parachute might reasonably
have been expected to save his life.' And he added: 'It being the
opinion of a good many senior officers and squadron commanders
that parachutes are not likely to be of any useful service on training
machines, the account of Lt Berkeley's death is appended.'

As the work of adaptation ground on, Everard Calthrop, inventor
of the Guardian Angel parachute, counted his losses: £20,000 and
an unreckonable sum in terms of exasperation. Released from the
obligatory wartime vow of silence, Calthrop issued in March 1919
an advertising brochure which was also a declaration of faith and
an exposé of official inertia. Never one for diplomatic finesse,
Calthrop laid into the Service Establishment with gusto and
obvious disgust, with the exception of officers such as the handful
of Maitlands and Orde-Leeses who had consistently championed
him in particular and the parachute in general. 'The work now
being done by the Parachute Committee and other departments
of the British Air Ministry,' Calthrop noted bitterly, 'is precisely
that which we continually begged the air authorities to undertake
from as far back as July 1916.' On the specific official view that
deaths in the air during training were inevitable, Calthrop said:
'It has apparently struck no one . . . of those professing to take a
special interest in the Air Force, to enquire into these casualties
to ascertain whether the means did not exist by which they might
be reduced.' Calthrop quotes a senior officer as saying, during the
war, 'We can't force a thing like this on our youngsters. If they want
it, they will ask for it,' a comment whose answer lies with many of
the 6,000 British Air Force dead. Just how many British pilots were
sacrificed on the altar of official lethargy over parachutes in that
war is impossible to say, but at least 250 are known to have hurled
themselves from their burning planes in last desperate attempts
to choose the quicker death. Countless others crashed with their
planes who might have survived had the parachute not been the
mistrusted and underdeveloped novelty it was.

Now, catching the heady mood of victory, the showmen got
busy again, among them William Newell, the first Englishman

to demonstrate a parachute jump from a moving aircraft, in 1914. He repeated his performance at Hendon, north London, on Whit Monday 1919, this time with two parachutes in case one was not impressive enough. In September he appeared in the role of hot air balloon stuntman at a Victory Sports display at Harrow, coupling a hair-raising act with a further double parachute drop. It was a performance worthy of the nineteenth-century aeronauts. Newell dug a long trench and covered it with iron sheeting and a layer of earth. At one end he lit a wood fire, from which the heat and smoke passed through into a balloon at the other. When the balloon filled with hot air, he perched on the sling of the attached-type parachute and was swept high into the air until he cut himself loose, opening one parachute and picturesquely descending on the second.

Women jumpers, such as the pretty nineteen-year-old Sylva Boyden, 'the English Air Girl', were still often in the public eye. Sylva was introduced to parachuting by Major Orde-Lees, who met her on an aero-engineering course at Chatham, taught her to jump and took her on demonstration tours of Scandinavia, the Continent, and America using the Guardian Angel. In 1919 Sylva made what was thought to be the first jump in Britain by a woman from a plane in flight when she parachuted from a Handley Page biplane during a display at Cricklewood, north London, and gave a jumping demonstration at the RAF's first air pageant at Hendon in 1920.

Lacking the momentum of war to carry them on, most nations let parachute research fall into abeyance. In Britain, Calthrop's was still regarded as the best parachute we had, even though it had not been officially adopted, and in May 1919 it enjoyed one brief hour of public glory. A Handley Page bomber zoomed in over Hyde Park (London), and dropped by parachute a bouquet of roses which were hastened by car to Marlborough House as a gift for Queen Alexandra. In the United States, Britain's lack of interest in the parachute idea was not shared – at least not by the Army, which was anxious to develop its Air Corps and conserve, through safety, the huge investment it made in each trainee. Ideas began to take physical shape late in 1918. The US Army earmarked funds for parachute development and in an old aircraft hangar at the McCook Flying Field, Dayton, Ohio, the work went ahead.

Major E. L. Hoffman, an aeronautical engineer, who took charge as military leader, quickly gathered around him a small team of zealots, including a veteran pilot, Floyd Smith, a brilliant technician who in 1910 had built his own aircraft and in 1914, as the result of a near-fatal accident, had been toying with the idea of a manually operated parachute pack. As the war progressed and the need for parachutes became evident, Smith became a dedicated enthusiast and willingly joined the team from his job in aircraft production engineering with the Army Air Service. His companions in the McCook team were Guy Ball, a former racing driver, James M. Russell (later to become famous for his unusual Lobe parachute), Jimmy Higgins, a former car salesman, and Sgt Ralph Bottriell, an army balloonist and parachutist. Although most of them had no experience whatever in parachute design, they generated tremendous energy, and it was at McCook that the modern parachute was born. Hoffman busied himself with a programme of dummy drops with existing parachutes garnered from all over the world, among them the Guardian Angel and the Mears from Britain, the Heinecke from Germany, the French FTA, made of cotton, the American AEF, and the French Robert. Rigorous tests, conducted under all types of conditions, ultimately led to one incontrovertible conclusion: that the attached-type parachute was inadequate for aircraft emergency use and should be abandoned. Apart from its bulk and discomfort, too much could go wrong: shroud lines could become entangled, canopies were too weak to withstand air pressure during deployment at high speed. Even under first-class conditions they proved unreliable and were consistently fouled by aircraft. So the McCook team drew up a list of stringent requirements which their ideal parachute should meet:

1. The parachute must make it possible for the airman to leave the aircraft regardless of the position it might be in when disabled.
2. The operating means must not depend on the airman falling from the aircraft.
3. The parachute equipment must be fastened to the body of the airman at all times while he is in the aircraft.
4. Operating the parachute must not be complicated; it must not be liable to foul or be susceptible to damage from any ordinary service conditions.
5. The parachute must be of such a size and be so disposed to give the maximum comfort to the wearer and allow him to leave the aircraft with the least possible difficulty or delay.
6. It must open promptly and be capable of withstanding

the shock of a 200lb (91kg) load falling at 400mph (644kph).

7. It must be reasonably steerable.

8. The harness must be comfortable and very strong, and designed so as to transfer the shock of opening without physical injury to the airman. It must be sufficiently adjustable to fit large and small people.

9. The harness must prevent the airman from falling out when the parachute opens, and it must be possible for him to remove quickly when landing in water or a high wind.

10. The strength of the 'follow through' must be uniform to the top of the parachute.

11. The parachute must be simple in construction and be easily packed with little time and labour.

Painstakingly, Hoffman, Russell, Smith, Ball, and a newcomer to the team, Leslie Leroy Irvin, picked their way through the problems towards a 100 per cent freefall parachute. They experimented with canopies ranging in diameter between 20ft (6m) and 34ft (10.4m), shaped the panels, and used a tough grade of silk that would stand up to increasing aircraft speeds. Into the apex they put a 3ft (1m) diameter flexible vent to soften the shock of opening and relieve the air pressure during deployment. They improved harnesses using strong webbing, and substituted braided silk rigging lines for hemp to make them more flexible and free from any tendency to twist. The result was the A-type freefall pack parachute. Pack flaps were flipped open by a system of elastic cords which were activated by a hand-operated ripcord, and a small auxiliary parachute, two feet in diameter, made the opening even more positive. The pilot or auxiliary parachute sat on the main one above the vent, with its own tiny rigging lines connecting to the parent and braced with steel ribs and powerful springs. Floyd Smith applied for a patent for such a parachute on 27 July 1918, and it was granted on 18 May 1920. The ripcord was attached to a ring on the wearer's chest, and also thread ties on the backpack.

The parachute showed up well in dummy tests and in April 1919 Major Hoffman decided it was time to try a live drop never before attempted with his freefall parachute. The choice of who should carry out the experiment fell on Irvin, a name to remember. Irvin, a short, well-built young man in his mid-twenties, was a parachute engineer with a varied but curiously single-minded background. Exactly how he reached the parachute 'laboratory' at McCook

Field is uncertain, for accounts vary in detail. But it seems that Major Hoffman, hearing of Irvin's interest and experience in the parachute field, invited him by letter to help in their researches. When Irvin first went along, he had with him an attached-type parachute of his own design, but was told that this system had been ruled out in favour of the freefall ripcord type. Thereupon he and Floyd Smith joined forces, and it was largely due to their efforts that the Type A prototype was produced.

Even as a boy Irvin had been fascinated by parachutes. A keen spectator at local carnivals, he would watch enthralled as jumps were made from hot air balloons in his home town, Los Angeles. One of his early exploits as a schoolboy was to make a large model balloon-and-parachute with a release mechanism that he had worked out himself. To the parachute, beneath the balloon, he attached a cat, which he sent soaring high over the city. Unfortunately for the cat the release mechanism failed to work, and it and the model balloon were wafted out to sea never to return. The experience led a chastened Irvin to a firm resolution: never again would he involve anyone but himself in his experiments. Having left school at fourteen, Irvin went to work for an aeroplane inventor, became an assistant to a stunt car driver (serving as ballast on fast corners), then balloonist with Universal Films and a high diver in circuses. It was his experience in the last role, leaping into a net, that convinced him that falling from a height did not, as had been widely believed for many a decade, cause a man to lose consciousness or control. At the age of sixteen Irvin persuaded a circus proprietor to let him stand in for an umbrella jumper, Capt Campbell, who had to abandon his act because of illness. With his father's permission, Irvin did so, and stayed with the circus for three years. As time went on he increased the height of the jump and the size of the umbrella. Eventually he was experimenting with parachutes and, billed as 'Ski-Hi Irvin', was soon performing balloon drops throughout his home state of California. Later, though it took a sweetener to induce the pilot to take him up, Irvin made a jump from an aircraft with a parachute stuffed in a sack under the cockpit, one of the earliest jumps ever made from a plane. It was an attached-type parachute; a manually operated one was still a dream. During World War I, Irvin worked for the Curtiss Aeroplane Co. at Buffalo, New York, spending much of his time designing and making his parachute. When completed, the prototype was about 32ft (9.6m) in diameter, had twenty-four silk rigging lines and a two-and-a-half-foot diameter pilot parachute. Late in 1918 he tried it out repeatedly with a life-sized dummy from an aircraft, attaching a static line to tug the ripcord as it fell. It landed safely every time. It was sad that this did not match up to the McCook criteria, but the freefall A-type that he and Floyd Smith then produced certainly did. At 28ft (8.5m) in diameter, it was smaller than Irvin's, but was similar in other respects.

On 19 April 1919, while his young wife Velda waited apprehensively at their Los Angeles home with his three-year-old daughter, Irvin made history at McCook Field by jumping from a DH 4 biplane with a freefall manually operated ripcord parachute. He carried his parachute on his back, with a harness specially designed to brace his whole body so as to spread the shock of opening; over his shoulders went the webbing, round his waist, under his legs and up the front of his body, with connector hooks at chest and thighs. He carried a second parachute as a reserve; this was a concession to pessimists who were convinced that a ripcord parachute would fail, but Irvin was equally convinced that it wouldn't. Floyd Smith was the pilot. He took the DH 4 up to 1,500ft (457m) and came in smoothly for a level run at 100mph (161kph). Irvin gave Smith a farewell wave and vanished over the side, snatching the ripcord as he fell. By the time he had dropped 1,000ft (305m) the parachute was fully blown, and he floated down with only one mishap to mar the fall: in his excitement he landed badly and broke an ankle. What he had not done was to break his neck, as many feared he would. Nor had he become unconscious. And the success of the manually operated parachute now seemed assured. In the following weeks many more jumps were made, and the US Army, satisfied with the results, then turned to the matter of contracts. In June 1919 Irvin was given his first order for 300 parachutes and found he had now become a parachute manufacturer and businessman.

A month later occurred the first major disaster involving the traditional attached-type parachutes, though they were not the cause. On 21 July the dirigible airship *Wing Foot Express*, built principally to publicise the rubber company which owned it, set off on a test flight over Chicago carrying a pilot, John A. Boettner, mechanics Henry Wacker and Buck Weaver, Earl Davenport (a publicity man) and Milton G. Norton, a press photographer. At five in the afternoon, about 1,200ft (366m) up, the dirigible suddenly buckled in half in a huge mass of flame. All in the airship except Davenport jumped with their parachutes, but only three survived. Weaver's parachute was immediately burnt to a fragment by the wreckage, and he fell to his death on nothing but rigging lines. Wacker's caught fire too, but luckily the rush of air as he descended snuffed out the flames. Boettner's began to burn, but he landed before it properly caught fire, and Norton, who started down well, landed up against a building and fell to the street, fatally injured. The wreckage of the airship wrought dreadful havoc down below. It sank down on a large bank building, its engine and fuel tank smashing into a section where girl typists and filing clerks worked. All told, the disaster killed thirteen people and injured thirty others, but despite an inquiry the cause of the fire itself remained a mystery.

Although the McCook team were happy with the new ripcord parachute, they continued to experiment with static-line models if only to prove that they had exhausted every possibility. It was during these experiments that a young RAF officer from England, Lt R.A. Caldwell, helped in a tragic way to vindicate their opting for the ripcord parachute. Caldwell had gone out to McCook with Major Orde-Lees to demonstrate Calthrop's static-line Guardian Angel. On the day of the jump the parachute was fixed as usual beneath the plane's fuselage, the attachment rope snaking up to Caldwell in one of the cockpits. The plane climbed to about 900ft (274m), and then Caldwell jumped. Interest among the spectators turned to consternation as they saw poor Caldwell dangling helplessly beneath the plane, his static line hooked up on an elevator rocker arm. In seconds it was cut through and Caldwell, trailing frayed rope, plummeted to earth and in five seconds was dead. As far as the Americans were concerned, any hopes retained for the attached-type parachute died with him.

During later tests on other parachutes, an incident occurred that gave Irvin immense satisfaction. In August 1920, LeRoy B. Jahn, a fellow American, went along to demonstrate his new quick-opening packet which incorporated four enormous springs, each about four feet (1.2m) long. These were stitched into the parachute's skirt or periphery to help deployment, and were compressed to about a foot long when packed. After slightly modifying the design, Jahn sought to prove its reliability from a plane using an employee, William O'Connor, as the jumper. With the memory of Caldwell's fatal drop still sickeningly fresh, the McCook men were disinclined to take any more chances; they insisted that Jahn's man should carry a standard Irvin in reserve. Jahn took great exception to this, accusing them of insulting his own design. But the Army was firm: the Irvin in addition or the demonstration was off. Reluctantly,

O'Connor donned the Irvin as well as the Jahn, and jumped from 2,000ft (610m). For 1,500ft (457m) he dropped like lead, his Jahn parachute flapping uselessly above his head, entangled with the giant springs. Quickly, O'Connor pulled the ripcord of the Irvin – and landed alive.

After 50,000 test jumps, the Army Air Corps made the wearing of parachutes compulsory. The decision was triggered by the death of Lt F.W. Niedermeyer, who one day forgot to put on the parachute he usually wore. He was taking part in combat practice with a friend when his plane collapsed in mid-air, throwing him out from sufficient height to kill him.

For Leslie Irvin, the date of 20 October 1922 was to be a historic one. In the afternoon, Lt Harold R. Harris, an experienced pilot, was flying a Loening plane to continue tests with partly balanced ailerons. The aircraft had been flown the previous day and had given no trouble, but as he flew over Dayton, Ohio he spotted another aircraft flown by a Lt Fairchild, and both began air fighting practice. During this bout, Harris lost control of the plane which began to dive so fast that chunks of wing fell off. Realising it was doomed, Harris unclipped his safety belt, stood up and was swept up and out of the cockpit. As he spun down he pulled what he thought was the ripcord of the parachute, but to his dismay nothing happened. Three times he tugged away, with the same result. Then he realised that what he had been pulling was part of his leg harness. After 1,800ft (549m) of freefall, he found the ripcord ring and the parachute opened at about 700ft (213m) from the ground. It was his first jump ever, and the first real aircraft emergency drop to have been made with the Irvin. Harris became the first Serviceman member of that large but exclusive coterie called the Caterpillar Club, which over the years would 'recruit' many thousands of flyers who had saved their lives using an Irvin-type parachute.

Chapter Nine

Parachutes for All

In the early 1920s another parachute emerged as a rival to the Irvin. This was from the inventive mind of Col H. E. S. Holt. So far he had devised a flare dispenser, an acetylene burner to help aircraft to land, a gadget for dropping mailbags from aircraft, and a suit with large pockets for pilots to house a parachute and its auxiliary, released with a timing device. Now he had produced a freefall parachute, one similar to many being marketed in the United States. He claimed it was much safer than attached-type parachutes because it would more likely open when a plane was diving steeply and when the differences in speeds between the jumper and the aircraft might be insufficient to tug an attached-type from its housing on the plane. Although it was being studied at the RAF's experimental station at Orfordness (Suffolk), Holt criticised the RAF parachute section for being 'obsessed' with trying to find a parachute system which would function when used from a plane flying normally, under control. 'But . . . who wants to escape from a machine flying normally, under control?' he asked. The automatic type, like the Guardian Angel, no doubt functioned beautifully under ordinary conditions, said the Colonel, but it was a death-trap if used from a machine which had crumpled in mid-air – unless the pilot fell faster than the machine and could haul the parachute out.

As for the Guardian Angel itself, its days were drawing to a close. Its poor inventor Calthrop was still making little headway with officialdom, though he continued to have an influential and forceful ally in Major Orde-Lees. In February 1920, in *Flight* magazine, Orde-Lees took issue with Col Holt, pressing his case again for the Guardian Angel, arguing that when he used an attached-type his pulse rate shot up from 56 to 112, but with what he called a 'problematical' opener, i.e. a ripcord parachute, it went even further – to 129. 'Let any of the positive-opening-no-use experts come forward and jump from any low height,' he wrote, 'and I'll undertake, because I've done it already, to go one lower in altitude every time with a positive-opener.' But for all his consistent devotion to the Guardian Angel and his loyalty to Calthrop, he failed to answer Holt's valid and fundamental objection to the Guardian Angel, that unless the pilot of a stricken plane drops faster than the plane itself, he will hardly haul an attached-type parachute from its fixed position under the fuselage. There is a real risk that it would not have positively opened at all.

In Parliament, the abortive question-and-answer game went on. In May 1919 the Air Ministry had been urged to amend the Civil Air regulations and make parachutes compulsory. The Air Ministry spokesman, Maj-Gen J. E. B. Seely, said predictably that the question was receiving 'close attention', but 'development had not at present reached the stage in which compulsory universal provision would be either practical or advantageous for military or civil aviation'. A little later, Mr Baldwin Raper MP, a former war pilot, tried his 15st (95kg) weight on a Guardian Angel from a Handley Page aircraft at 600ft (183m) to get first-hand information of the value and efficiency of parachutes. Even this burden was no trouble to the Guardian Angel, which gave him a soft landing. It was Mr Raper who elicited the interesting information in Parliament in July 1921 that the RAF then had 1,943 parachutes, but fitting, it surprised nobody to hear, had been delayed because of difficulties over harness design. A few planes and one balloon were equipped: 'Experiments are proceeding and satisfactory results are expected shortly.'

The early 1920s were depressing years for parachute advocates, largely because, now the war was over and there was a general preoccupation with peacetime problems, what little will there had been during the war had melted away. In August 1921 they lost one of the most devoted workers in the cause of air safety, former President of the Parachute Committee and the first man to jump successfully from an airship in flight: Air Commodore (as he now was) E. M. Maitland. Ironically, Maitland was killed in the R38 airship disaster, when forty-four people out of forty-nine died. They were equipped with parachutes, but no one had a chance to use them; one of the five survivors, Harry Bateman of the National Physical Laboratory, said the suddenness of the disaster gave them no time. Only a few seconds elapsed between the airship's buckling and its dive into the river Humber. The following year William Newell, the first person to jump from an aircraft in flight in Britain, died too, and through his own carelessness – surprisingly for so experienced a parachutist. He omitted to make an essential adjustment to his parachute, and part of the canopy remained lodged in the container. The plane's pilot did his best to save him, flying down 60ft (18m) over water so that Newell could release himself and fall without injury. Newell certainly dropped, but after swimming only 60ft (18m) drowned while suffering from cold and exhaustion.

Meanwhile, Britain's airmen were still without parachutes, and Capt Frederick Guest, the Air Secretary, announced in the Commons that no fighting aircraft were fitted with them. No practice or experimental drops were being permitted from heavier-than-air craft, though 140 parachutes had been issued for Avro trainers, and the need for any modifications and improvements would be reported on. The position was thus practically stagnant. Rumours spread that the parachute research department was being depleted, and officers were said to be leaving. Was this true, asked Sir William Joynson Hicks in the Commons? 'I hope not,' replied Capt Guest, and hastened away to find out. A week later he wrote to Sir William admitting that yes, the separate research section had indeed closed down, in the interests of economy. There was no intention to abandon research on parachutes, he said, but this would be carried out by another department.

If research did continue, it led nowhere at all. It was three years before Capt Guest's successor, Sir Samuel Hoare, made the long awaited, long overdue announcement about parachute provision. The question of air safety appliances was now so urgent, Sir Samuel told MPs in March 1925, that they could wait no longer for a satisfactory type to be produced in Britain. The RAF would therefore be equipped with the parachute made by Leslie Irvin in the United States. Two thirds of the initial order of 2,261 would be imported; the balance, and all future supplies, would be made in Britain. So it was that Irvin came to England and in 1926 founded his factory at Letchworth (Herts) where, as Irvin Aerospace, a division of the Hunting group, it flourishes to this day. Irvin's contract was a blow for Col Holt, whose Autochute resembled the Irvin in many respects. He had demonstrated an early version not long after the decision to equip the RAF with the Irvin, a parachute which he claimed had embodied several features he had previously abandoned. The Autochute was a seatpack ripcord type like the Irvin, and it had a pilot parachute, also like the Irvin, which was released either by the pilot himself or automatically.

Some Autochute models had a third parachute between the pilot and the main canopy to reduce the shock of opening. The rigging lines were ingeniously stored in silk tubes to prevent entanglement. It was demonstrated at Stag Lane aerodrome in November 1925 by Capt H. Spencer, a parachutist who had made over 100 drops. He dived from a DH 9 head-first at 1,000ft (305m) and made a perfect landing. But the telling factor in favour of the Irvin was its proven value in the United States after 1918. It was to earn Major Hoffman, of McCook Field, the important Collier Trophy for 'the most distinguished contribution to the science of flight' for his work to perfect a freefall parachute.

The introduction of the Irvin parachute into Britain hit, more than anyone, Everard Calthrop, who had invested so much money, so much energy, patriotism and sheer compassion for the risk-ridden wartime pilots in his attached-type Guardian Angel that when he died in 1927 it was as a deeply disappointed man. The only fruits of his years of dogged effort were two honours from the Italian government (the Guardian Angel had been used with distinction on the Italian front in World War I) and estate worth £1,777.

Among Hoffman's team at McCook, it will be recalled, was James M. Russell, who devised two interesting parachutes, one of which competed for government approval in England. Russell, after being asked by Hoffman to make a parachute providing 'positive opening', produced the Valve, which had been patented in 1924. This had no vent in the apex, but instead featured valve-like openings in the overlapping parts of the canopy's panels. For various reasons it was never used, but it led Russell to design another and more important model, the uniquely shaped Lobe. Russell recognised that the development of the parachute had been concentrated on the pack, harness and method of attachment or deployment; the canopy itself had changed little fundamentally from the mushroom it had always been. Even the Irvin maintained this tradition. Russell claimed that both the spring in the Irvin pilot parachute and the elastic in the pack which hastened its opening were affected by climatic conditions, and needed to be repacked. Moreover, he felt, the pilot parachute might foul and not pull the main one from the pack; shroud lines might become twisted; and below 200ft (61m) performance was variable. With the Lobe, Russell hoped to overcome the principal weakness of other parachutes, including the Valve – namely, a tendency to oscillate, the curse of parachute jumping since Garnerin's nauseous jumps over Paris and London from 1797. Russell's answer was to dispense with the pilot parachute, flatten the canopy and turn the edge under in a wide curve. Oscillation almost vanished, and he also achieved quicker opening by modifying the pack so that it could open horizontally.

The new Lobe created quite a stir when it was tested in 1927. The shock on opening was a mere one third of that of other parachutes, but there was a tendency for the shroud lines to hook over the canopy when it opened. Two young test jumpers cured this by a continuous and dangerous process of trial and error, leaping in such a way as to foul the parachute deliberately. When the backpack was improved the trouble stopped. Russell was joined as demonstrator by John Tranum, a Danish-born stuntman whose repertoire during barnstorming days in the United States included such feats as playing tennis with a partner on the wing of a plane in flight, wing-walking, and transferring from one aircraft to another in mid-flight. He came to England to help set up a factory for Russell, to be built with American capital but employing British labour. His introduction to parachuting had come about on a day when the scheduled jumper at a display field failed to turn up. He was offered fifty dollars to make a jump, asked for sixty and got it. In the US he had been one of a large corps of airborne acrobats who proliferated in post-war America, many of them former World War I pilots whose skill, flying, was not enough to guarantee them other work. So they bought up hundreds of redundant war planes and set the country buzzing in the only way they knew.

Some of the acts were bizarre. One flying circus jumper who had the crowd on the edge of their seats was Buddy Plunkett, a veteran who made his first parachute jump at the age of fourteen. He was a master of a neat piece of sleight-of-hand in which he would make a long freefall drop with a visibly torn parachute, and then, when only a few hundred feet above the ground, tug the ripcord on a genuine parachute. Plunkett and Tranum became involved with Hollywood film-makers' passion for re-enacting aerial dogfights of World War I. This pair were among several required to perform the stunt of jumping from a plane that had been soaked in petrol and oil. One of Tranum's stunts was parachuting from the bridge at Pasadena 154ft (47m) over the so-called river, the Arroyo Seco ('dry gulch'), in California, a venue better known for suicides than stunt jumpers. After coming to England, Tranum met Everard Calthrop and negotiated supplies of fabric. Tranum's view of Calthrop was patronising: he thought his factory well organised, but dismissed his parachute as a typical product of a railway engineer. Russell's Lobe parachute was intended primarily for commercial use, but Tranum tried hard to catch the interest of the Air Ministry. They liked the Lobe, but considered it no better than the Irvin they had already adopted, and saw no reason to change.

Tranum was one of the greatest stunt jumpers of all time. He was utterly fearless, and fully lived up to his confident visiting card slogan, 'Aerial stunts to order'. But he was sensitive, too, to the more aesthetic delights of parachute jumping – the silent solitude as he dangled in space, with only a gentle distant murmur of activity to remind him that life was going on below. 'What a grand and glorious feeling,' he enthused in his autobiography *Nine Lives*. 'Here I was, all by myself, the machine going on in the distance above, below me hundreds of people like so many flies, all looking up. I marvelled at the wonderful stillness around me, only faint noises from the ground were reaching me, such as cows bellowing, dogs barking, and the roar of excitement from the crowd, and I cascading down through golden sunshine on a long regular slant towards the earth.' When Major Orde-Lees jumped into the Thames he was using the attached-type Guardian Angel, but when Tranum repeated the performance he used a ripcord type already opened out, and he dived in off the top of his parked car. He was always game for anything. Once, for a film company, he had driven a motorcycle with a parachute attached over a cliff. As soon as it was airborne he opened the parachute, let the motorcycle crash, and landed unharmed in a 1,000ft (305m) deep canyon below. One day Tranum made an attempt to upstage a stunter named Simpson whose personal speciality was a long drop of 1,000 or 2,000ft (305 or 710m) before letting out his parachute, which he held in his arms. Simpson's big mistake was to assume that the current of air would necessarily be upwards. When he threw out the canopy, it was blown against him and he dropped from 6,000ft (1,830m) to within a few hundred feet of the ground before the parachute, which had wrapped itself round him like the shroud it almost became, blew open. Tranum's solution was to experiment with the idea that had killed the unfortunate Cocking nearly a century before. Tranum used an ordinary non-rigid parachute, attached a cord to the apex inside the canopy and then hauled it down to convert it almost into an inverted cone. The effect, as he pulled on the cord, was to reduce the drag and speed up his descent; only when he approached the ground did he let go the central cord and slow himself to a safe speed. Tranum also specialised in delayed drops, timing his freefall with a stopwatch as he went. But it was the prelude to one of these attempts that was to be the death of him. On 7 March 1935, after reluctantly yielding to pressure, he was taken up in a plane from Kastrup airport in Copenhagen. His object was not only to break his own 17,250ft (5,261m) freefall record, but to beat a Russian's subsequent 25,000ft (7,625m) drop and create a new world 'first' of 30,000ft (9,150m). During the flight over the city, and at about 27,000ft (8,235m), Tranum suddenly began gesticulating wildly to the pilot who, realising something was amiss, took the plane down as quickly as he could. Tranum had collapsed in his seat, and doctors spent hours trying to resuscitate him, but in vain. After a lifetime of tempting a merciful Providence, the jumper had died from a heart attack – not at all the kind of death he might have chosen for himself.

Like their nineteenth-century forerunners, Tranum and his fellow stunt jumpers may have performed mainly for thrills (and money), but their jumps did, indirectly, add to the sum total of aviation knowledge. For example, parachute experts who watched their antics learned something about the limits of human endurance in the air, and thus about what could be expected of the parachute and the man. The myth that the speed of a freefall descent would lead to unconsciousness was exploded by Irvin and others, and it had also been established that, far from a man falling at 250mph (402kph), as was widely thought, the normal speed would be little more than 120mph.

One of the daredevils of the 1920s who came to value the emergency parachute was Charles A. Lindbergh, who having learned to fly after World War I for a time toured the US in a barnstorming role making exhibition jumps. But later he was to achieve world fame by becoming the first flyer to make a solo non-stop flight across the Atlantic. He was twenty-five when he performed this feat, flying from Long Island to Paris in his plane *The Spirit of St Louis* on 20/21 May 1927. Four times he was to save his life by parachute. The first occasion was in 1924 when he joined the US Army. He had his first taste of danger at Kelly Field, Texas while taking part in a mock attack on a bomber. Lindbergh, in company with another plane piloted by a Lt McCallister, in the top unit of a formation of nine SE5s, was converging on a DH 4B at about 5,000ft (1,525m). He recounted what ensued in an official report, quoted in his book *We – Pilot and Plane.*

Wartime supply dropping, using a quadruple parachute cluster. *(The Times)*

'Remember, a man's life depends . . .' WAAF parachute packers at Ringway during World War II. *(Imperial War Museum)*

Saved by his ejection seat: a dramatic bale-out by the pilot of a Lightning jet. *(Daily Mirror.*

The ejection seat is blasted off during a test on a Martin-Baker test rig. Some zero/zero seats reach twice the height of Nelson's Column. *(Martin-Baker)*

Ejection seat designer and engineer the late Sir James Martin. He developed a means of saving 6,500 aircrew in high-speed planes. *(Martin-Baker)*

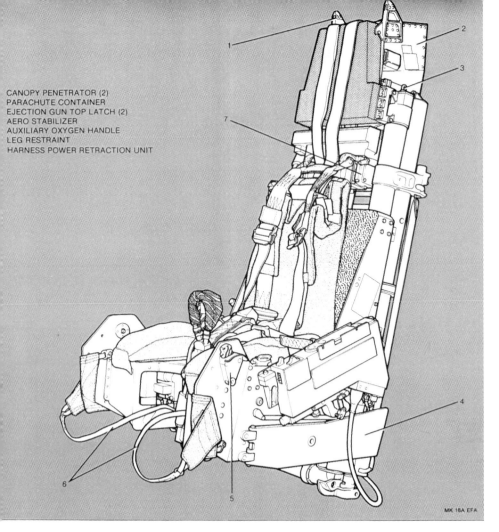

CANOPY PENETRATOR (2)
PARACHUTE CONTAINER
EJECTION GUN TOP LATCH (2)
AERO STABILIZER
AUXILIARY OXYGEN HANDLE
LEG RESTRAINT
HARNESS POWER RETRACTION UNIT

MK 16A EFA

Drawing showing parts of an ejection seat. *(Martin-Baker)*

An Avro Vulcan jet plane is braked to a
stop with an RFD-GQ parachute.

he parachute that failed . . . In 1971, Apollo 15's spacecraft landed on only two of its ant parachutes – the other collapsed. *(NASA)*

smoke jumper, one of 400 in the nited States, makes a hazardous mp to investigate a forest fire. *S Forest Service)*

Tracy Rixon, with her French Papillo
parachute, touches down during th
1972 British National Parachu
Championships in which she won th
women's title. *(Daily Telegraph)*

Over-water parascending with a round
parachute from a tow boat makes an
exciting seaside holiday highlight.
(Barry Clark)

...y-diving: the Red Devils Freefall Team form a seven-man star over Cyprus. *(Red Devils)*

Up and away . . .Training prospective overland parascenders with a truck tow at South Cerney airfield (Glos.), using the mattress-like manoeuvrable ram-air parachute.
(John Lucas)

Watch this space . . . In October 1997 a mission to Titan, Saturn's biggest moon, leaves Earth to begin its seven-year

I passed above the DH and a moment later felt a slight jolt. My head was thrown forward against the cowling and my plane seemed to turn around and hang nearly motionless for an instant. I closed the throttle and saw an SE5 with Lt McCallister in the cockpit a few feet away on my left. He was apparently unhurt and getting ready to jump. Our ships were locked together with fuselages approximately parallel. My right wing was damaged and folded back slightly, covering the forward right-hand corner of his cockpit. Then the ships started to mill around and the wires began whistling. The right wing started vibrating and striking my head at the bottom of each oscillation. I removed the rubber band safe-tying the belt, unbuckled it, climbed out past the trailing edge of the damaged wing and with my feet on the cowling on the right side of the cockpit, which was then in a nearly vertical position, I jumped backward as far from the ship as possible.

I had no difficulty in locating the pull-ring and experienced no sensation of falling. The wreckage was falling nearly straight down and for some time I fell in line with its path. Fearing the wreckage might fall on me, I did not pull the ripcord until I had dropped several hundred feet into the clouds. During this time I had turned one-half revolution and was falling flat and nearly face downwards. The parachute functioned perfectly; almost as soon as I pulled the ripcord, the riser jerked on my shoulders, the straps tightened, my head went down and the chute was fully opened. I saw Lt McCallister floating above me and the wrecked ships about 100 yards [91m] to one side, continuing to spin to the right and leave a trail of lighter fragments along their path. I watched them until, still locked together, they crashed ... about 2,000ft [610m] below and burst into flames several seconds after impact.

McCallister came down safely, and Lindbergh landed unhurt on the edge of a ditch after losing his goggles, a camera and the ripcord of the parachute.

Lindbergh made his second parachute escape when he took a new plane up for testing. He had not intended to wear a parachute at all, but the duty officer of the day had insisted, and within ten minutes Lindbergh had abundant reason to thank him. He put his plane into a spin at 2,500ft (762m) and could not pull out. So he jumped, at a mere 300ft (91m), and was fortunate enough to survive. His third and fourth escapes were in 1926 after he had become an Air Mail pilot. He found himself in fog while flying at night between St Louis and Chicago, with his petrol running out rapidly. He baled out 'blind' at 5,000ft (1,525m), with a flashlamp in his belt. Soon after he jumped he heard the engine of his plane start up again very near his descending parachute. The plane shot past him and crashed two miles away. Two months later, Lindbergh jumped for the last time – at a record 13,000ft (3.965m), in snow. He finished up on a barbed-wire fence, but apart from scratches suffered no injury. Later he flew out to collect the mail bag, which had dropped undamaged, and brought it back.

In the 1920s, Irvin established his famous Caterpillar Club for those who have saved their lives making emergency jumps by parachute. Lindbergh was the first member of it to make four life-saving jumps – a record until equalled in World War II during the Battle of Britain. The Caterpillar Club still thrives as an exclusive association, administered by Irvin but open to those who have saved their lives making an emergency jump using any Irvin or Irvin-designed parachute. The badge of membership is a small gilt caterpillar pin with tiny ruby-red eyes, and a certificate signed personally by Leslie Irvin, and later, until her death, by his widow Velda. A similar pin is presented to each Caterpillar even today. Although the first member was William O'Connor (see Chapter 8), who saved his life at McCook Field in 1920, he was a 'one-off'. His main parachute was a Jahn, which he intended to demonstrate, and his reserve, which he used because the Jahn failed, was an Irvin. So O'Connor only scraped into the club. Irvin made it clear in 1924 that nobody was eligible for Caterpillar Club membership who climbed into a plane with the intention of baling out – which O'Connor did. The second member, the first true Caterpillar, was Lt Harold R. Harris of the US Army Air Service over Dayton, Ohio in 1922. The Caterpillar Club will be described further in a later chapter. Suffice now to mention the apt significance of the badge itself. The caterpillar, or silkworm, was chosen by Irvin a few days after Harris's escape, and represents life hanging by a thread from the canopy of a parachute – at that time made of silk.

Chapter Ten

Prelude to War

It was not long before the advantages of the ripcord parachute became clear even to firm believers in the old attached type. In May 1925, shortly after the Air Ministry had approved the Irvin and decided to adopt it for the RAF, Major Orde-Lees, doughty campaigner for the Guardian Angel attached-type parachute, publicly turned his coat. He wrote in *The Times* that he himself would have recommended this type for pilots: 'Long experience has brought me gradually to the conclusion that [the freefall type] is likely to save more lives in the long run owing to its freedom from any possibility of fouling the machine, provided that the ripcord of the knapsack in which it is contained is not pulled too soon ... Parachutes will not save every life, of course, but they will give us a sporting chance, which we never had before. During the war a high percentage of German aviators were saved by their parachutes. We sacrificed about 8,000 lives for want of parachutes. At least 4,000 of those aviators could have been saved.' [Author's note: 8,000 appears to be an exaggeration; the figure quoted by the official history, *War in the Air* by H. A. Jones (OUP, 1937), is 6,000.] What Calthrop's feelings were at such a radical change of mind by a champion such as Orde-Lees can only be conjectured; nevertheless, not everyone agreed with Orde-Lees. Later that month, opponents of the freefall type felt vindicated when a young airman, Cpl Sydney Wilson of No. 12 Squadron RAF, lost his nerve in a first-time jump and failed to use either his main or reserve parachute and was killed. That is what happens, admonished the anti-freefall school, when you place too great an onus on the jumper, such as having to pull the ripcord. Consternation by the public led to questions in the Commons and for a time scepticism was renewed.

It was an accident involving a civilian that emphasised the lethal consequences of lack of parachute training or sound equipment, and led to an Air Ministry regulation aimed specifically at civilians.

99

It occurred at Leicester on 9 September 1926 when Capt A. F. Muir, an aircraft pilot who had been giving exhibition flights, conducting passenger trips and organising parachute descents, took up a would-be jumper, twenty-five-year-old Mrs Dorothy Cain. Earlier in the week several trouble-free jumps had been made with an attached-type parachute – the one being used by Mrs Cain. Having fitted the harness on her, the pilot flew her up to 1,000ft (305m) and gave the signal to jump. The crowd of 40,000 below saw Mrs Cain emerge from the plane and leap into space. But immediately came the agonising realisation that she was not wearing a parachute at all. Somehow it had become detached from her body and could be seen trailing from its case beneath the fuselage. Her distant figure, spreadeagled as she fell, thudded to earth and she was killed instantly – and before the eyes of her watching husband, who was in the crowd. For him it was a bitter shock. For several frustrating days he had been trying to convince her that it was unwise to make a jump at all.

Four days after this tragedy, the Air Ministry reacted with a ban on descents from civil aircraft unless permitted by directions issued by the Secretary of State. Applications for a jump had to be made fourteen days in advance. Parachutes were soon compulsory in the French air force; in the RAF, too, airmen were being trained in their use. And they had to be able to pack their parachutes before they made practice jumps. From 1926 onwards all new British aircraft were designed to accommodate seat-pack parachutes. A parachute training unit was formed at Henlow (Beds), where young airmen were schooled in jumping, first with a couple of 'pull-off' falls from a Vickers Vimy at about 500ft (152m). This meant standing on a specially built platform on one of the bracing struts between the wings, drawing the parachute ripcord and letting the wind fill out the canopy. The pull-off invariably followed, and in any struggle for second thoughts the parachute always won. Later, there followed a freefall jump from about 3,000ft (915m). Parachutes were compulsory for aircraft test pilots too. One of the side benefits of this was that testing could be pushed to the limits of an aircraft's performance without serious risk to life. In Copenhagen, for example, a pilot commissioned to discover the cause of a Fokker's break-up in the air put his machine into a steep dive at 9,000ft (2,745m) and when the wings broke up, jumped to safety before the machine crashed.

Attempts were made in Britain on behalf of various parachute types, such as Russell's Lobe, to interest the Services, but without success. One candidate was an Italian parachute, the Salvator, invented by an Italian officer and adopted by his country's air force. The Salvator could be used either with a static line or as a free type by operating a hand grip on the belt instead of a ripcord. It had an excellent safety record, and demonstrations at Hendon impressed British officials. But again, the Irvin had pre-empted it. Later, the Salvator was adopted by air forces in Japan, Spain and Switzerland. General Guidoni, the former Italian air attaché in London, was killed when experimenting with the Salvator, though the parachute could hardly be blamed. During a test at 3,000ft (915m), the General pulled the belt lever and jumped simultaneously without ensuring he was clear of the aircraft. The rigging lines tangled and the canopy did not deploy.

By the end of 1928, the Irvin parachute was becoming widely popular. After only two years it was being used in twenty-seven countries, and at Letchworth production had reached thirty-five parachutes a week, all for the RAF, compared with fifty a week by the parent company in Buffalo, USA. At his Letchworth factory, Leslie Irvin gave his employees a useful object lesson when one of his demonstrators jumped from a de Havilland monoplane piloted by Irvin himself. Seeing a parachute in action was a new experience for most of them. By the end of 1930, the Fleet Air Arm was equipped throughout with the Irvin quick-release parachute, whose central fitting was turned ninety degrees and allowed four attachment points to disengage simultaneously so that pilots could get free in water. Several other types of parachute were now available, including a 'form fitting' pack for use in aircraft cabins which slipped into the shape of the upholstery. But the seat pack remained standard. Irvin calculated that two lives were being saved for every hundred parachutes sold; until then 20,000 of their parachutes had been made and used.

Descents were being made from higher and higher altitudes . . . 16,000ft (4,880m), 18,000ft (5,490m), and then 24,000ft (7,320m) by a German airwoman, Frau Schröter, in 1932. Such feats attracted considerable public interest, far more than the fact that enthusiasm for parachuting had quickened in Russia. A mere 100 jumps were made there in 1930, 600 in 1931 and 2,000 in 1932. Within the next three years, 1,300 parachute clubs and more than 100 centres had sprung up, well-equipped and provided with training towers. But it was healthy revolutionary thinking in Russia that leisure should also be functional. A booklet issued by the People's Commissariat of Public Health talked of the importance of parachute jumping in

101

developing courage, resourcefulness, willpower, the ability not to panic in an emergency, and to make prompt decisions in the case of complications. It quoted the People's Commissar of Defence, Comrade Klimenti Efremovich Voroshilov (whose name was later to be familiar to the British as moderniser of the Red Army and President of the Soviet Union after Stalin's death in 1953): 'At the present time parachuting in the USSR has become a sport for the masses. In many towns there are parachute jumping towers. In factories, works and attached to aviation clubs there exist parachute jumping groups where young people learn this interesting job. This type of sport is of considerable importance for defence ... I must tell you, comrades, that this parachute business, one of the most complicated and delicate technical arts, is perfected not only as a sport and training in fortitude, but also as an important branch of our fighting strength.' As far back as 1927, thanks to the idea of a single officer, the Russians had dropped eight men behind 'enemy' lines during manoeuvres. In similar exercises in the 1930s, Russian troops swung down by parachute in their thousands, impressing such British top brass as Maj-Gen (later Field Marshal) Archibald Wavell, but apparently not strongly enough for him to urge the formation of paratroop units in Britain. The Russians also practised delayed drops. In 1937, Lt Kaytanov, an air force officer, was flown up to 36,000ft (10,980m), dropping to 4,000ft (1,220m) before he opened his parachute – and setting a world record.

In England, a new personality appeared on the parachute scene who was to have an indirect but profound effect on warfare in 1939–45: Raymond Quilter, son of Sir Cuthbert Quilter, a rich Suffolk baronet. Raymond was a one-time Guards officer, a keen amateur aviator who flew his own plane at Brooklands, and a parachute jumper. He had a restless, questing mind and was seldom satisfied with the status quo. Like Irvin, who had by now settled in England and with whom he later became a close personal friend, Quilter enjoyed expensive living. When his pleasures palled he sought other outlets for his energies, and encountered James Gregory, an extrovert enthusiast with a considerable parachute background. Gregory had started as a member of the first parachute section of the RAF in 1919, later becoming works manager for Calthrop at his Guardian Angel factory, and then for the Russell Parachute Company, makers of the Lobe. The parachutes currently used, Quilter and Gregory felt, were capable of much improvement, so they decided to make their own. Money was no problem. Arthur Dickinson, financial adviser to Sir Cuthbert Quilter, managed to persuade him to put up money for Raymond to buy silk fabric for parachutes. Dickinson joined the group to watch over his client's interests. The first few experimental emergency parachutes were made by Gregory and his wife on a sewing machine at home. By 1932, and from these small beginnings, Quilter and Gregory had designed a parachute to Air Ministry specifications, and one cheap enough to be within easy reach of a private flyer's pocket. It had a quick-acting pilot parachute, and the pack was padded with sponge rubber for comfort.

They were beginning to find lack of working space a serious hindrance until Reginald Dagnall came to their aid. Owner of the RFD company, which made, among other things, flotation gear to buoy up the wings of aircraft forced to land in the sea, Dagnall was sufficiently impressed by the Gregory–Quilter team to offer them a corner of his Guildford (Surrey) works, and to loan machinery. In 1934 the GQ company was formed, with Quilter, Dickinson and Dagnall as its first directors. The company aimed high from the start. They would compete with Irvin on his own ground and sell parachutes to the RAF, and cash in on the commercial aviation boom by providing a parachute for every passenger, targeting among others the moneyed young flyers who droned their weekends away over Brooklands. But the dream was more prosperous than the substance. Although GQ were allowed to tender to the Air Ministry, they were repeatedly rebuffed when it came to the point of actual orders. The Ministry could see no reason to disturb the exclusivity it had granted to Irvin. Nor were the civil airlines interested in GQ's products, on several grounds. Parachutes, they said, would add to a plane's weight; women would need to wear slacks to accommodate the harness, thus detracting from what was then regarded largely as a social event. And for passengers to be urged to wear parachutes would simply sow the seed of doubt about an aircraft's safety. Hardly, it was thought then, the right kind of marketing ploy. Moreover, with the increase in trans-Channel and transatlantic flying, the airlines did not want passengers throwing themselves into water in an emergency. They would rather they stayed with a plane when it landed on the sea, where flotation gear would keep it buoyant until rescue came. There was another factor. In the 1920s an admittedly small survey of twenty-six aircraft accidents showed that four in every five of them occurred on landing (35 per cent), approach (27 per cent) or take-off (19 per cent) – totalling 81 per cent. In all these cases a parachute would have been impracticable. GQ's plans to market a civil parachute came to naught. Hampered by lack of Air Ministry interest, GQ were compelled to tick over by making target plane drogues for their associate, Dagnall.

Then, in 1937, following a report from Lt-Gen Sir Andrew Thorne on German paratroop activity, GQ submitted to Leslie Hore-Belisha, Secretary of State for War, a scheme to use parachutes for troops. It was not accepted, but the Air Ministry nevertheless ordered fifty emergency parachutes for trials. The following June, at the opening of Luton airport, a German parachutist impressed the English crowd with a demonstration of the Eschner, a quick-opening parachute type which used a static line, had no pilot parachute and shot its canopy out by means of a spring. The intention was to show how easy it was to drop to the ground from an aircraft with an altitude as low as 150ft (45m). It was a hint that should have been heeded, particularly as the 1930s were already clouded by unease at Hitler's rise to power and Germany's aggressive expansionism in Europe. No action was taken until the Munich crisis in 1938 when the Chamberlain government was spurred into rearmament. With an eye to strengthening the RAF for possible warfare, GQ was asked: what is your potential? The company, only too keen for some potential, abandoned the old skating rink it had been renting at Woking, girded itself for business and built a new factory. The government, it was clear, was going to need all the planes, all the pilots and all the emergency parachutes it could get.

The factory at Woking was designed to make 24ft (7.3m) diameter emergency parachutes, though for some years Quilter and Gregory had been working on a design for a larger version, 28ft (8.5m) in diameter and with a static line for paratrooops. Quilter's uncle returned from a long sojourn in Germany during Hitler's military build-up, and there he had witnessed a paratroop demonstration which had much impressed him. What, he enquired of his nephew Raymond, was Britain doing in this area of activity? The answer was: nothing. Not long before, the Russians had made a drop of 1,200 men, 150 machine-guns and eighteen light field-guns by parachute and assembled them all in eight minutes. *Flight* magazine reported: 'It is felt in authoritative circles in Britain that although [the formation of paratroop units] might prove most useful in general second-class warfare in many parts of the world, it would not be a practical manoeuvre in modern

European warfare.' This view was an accurate expression of feeling among the European nations. Although the Russians had set the pace, followed to a lesser degree by the French, little headway was made – except by Germany. The Germans, having watched the Russians' progress in military manoeuvres, had been training paratroops and forming active units since as far back as 1935, two years after Hitler came to power. The first Russian paratroops used freefall parachutes, opened by the men themselves who were instructed not to pull their ripcords until they were within 1,000ft (305m) of the ground. The Germans, however, used static lines from aircraft, dropping at 200ft (61m) or even less.

That so little was known or noted about Germany's systematic paratroop preparedness is amazing. It was not kept secret, but even though Germany did not stage any displays, material was certainly published on the subject in Germany before the war. In the *Deutsche Allgemein Zeitung,* for example, Rear-Admiral Gadow wrote an article which quite openly discussed the possibility of an invasion of England, emphasising the use of an attack by paratroops; not only troops, but equipment and arms. By the time war was declared, on 3 September 1939, the Germans were leading all other nations in paratroop training, manpower, strategy and tactics, and paratroops became a key ingredient in their concept of *Blitzkrieg* ('lightning war'), as the countries of mainland Europe were soon to discover to their tragic cost.

CHAPTER ELEVEN

THE HEAVENS OPENED

In World War II the parachute served friend and foe in practically every theatre of war. It ushered stricken pilots to safety and airborne armies to victory and defeat, brought food and supplies to the hungry and flared the way for the bomber's havoc. As uses for the parachute widened, so did knowledge of its aerodynamics. It was recognised, for example, that every parachute has a critical opening speed in which the type of fabric and its porosity and weave, and the rate that air enters it, play a crucial part. For example, if a low-porosity fabric such as linen were used with air entering it at high speed, it could mean rapid opening, but a burst canopy. At the other extreme, a high-porosity material (such as cotton) with air entering slowly and escaping through the fabric could mean the parachute failing to develop, i.e. squidding. The skill and expertise of parachute technology began to be concerned with striking the fine balance between a parachute's fabric, porosity, opening speed, and the job it was intended to do. Experts at last came to appreciate why the parachutes of the pioneers, beginning with Garnerin in 1797, suffered such severe oscillation: because the fabric they used, usually canvas or heavy linen, was too impervious to air and caused oscillation as the air struggled to escape under the edges of the canopy.

Until 1939, silk was in general use for airmen's emergency parachutes. Two advantages of this are that a large canopy can be fitted into a small pack; it also has a high-tensile strength. But silk supplies quickly dried up when war came, and there was a feverish search for alternative materials, not only for emergency parachutes but to meet the many other needs: for paratroops, vehicle dropping, braking aircraft on short runways, and so on. During the war, arms and supplies were dropped with high-grade lightweight cotton parachutes, sometimes in clusters for increased stability and to cope with heavy loads. With the discovery of synthetic fibres such as nylon, the silk shortage became less crucial. Nylon, which does not deteriorate quickly, was introduced for RAF emergency parachutes and, along with cotton, for dropping paratroops. Jute hessian, a natural fibre, was put into service for sending down mines at sea. The Germans used heavy rayon parachutes for dropping explosives and, masters of *ersatz* and improvisation that they were, even developed an ingenious parachute woven from folded paper thread.

Before World War II there had been no air drops of British fighting men, though even as far back as 1918 the commander of the Americans' 1st Brigade in France, Col William Mitchell, was planning to parachute a whole infantry division behind enemy lines. Between the wars, the Russians and Germans had led the way with airborne exercises, and during Italy's conquest of Abyssinia in 1935–36 she was reported to have used her Salvator parachute for an air drop of goods including petrol, live animals, medical kits, and even a surgeon. Russia never made large-scale use of paratroops, and even during the war against Finland in late 1939 only comparatively few were dropped, possibly because the Finns were too loyal to provide a willing and useful fifth column. The parachute's first major military role came in May 1940 when Hitler invaded the Low Countries. His airborne troops, taking advantage of the flat terrain, were able to establish bridgeheads, create confusion, preoccupy the energies of the Dutch Army, and thrive on the willing aid of a fruitful supply of Dutch traitors. On 22 June, with France overrun and on the point of surrender and the Dunkirk withdrawal an ugly recent memory, Winston Churchill took a decisive step towards establishing a paratroop regiment. Only the previous month he had succeeded Neville Chamberlain as Prime Minister; now he wrote to his Chief of Staff: 'We ought to have a corps of at least 5,000 parachute troops . . . I hear something is being done already to form such a corps but only, I believe, on a very small scale. Advantage must be taken of the summer to train these forces, who can none-the-less play their part meanwhile as shock troops in home defence.'

A few weeks later, at the Manchester airport at Ringway, opened in 1938 and under operational control of the RAF, paratroop (and, later, glider troop) training began. RAF Ringway was also used for aircraft production and modification and trial flights by the Fairey and Avro aircraft companies. Many aircraft, including the famous Lancaster bomber, made their maiden flights here. It was opened first as the Central Landing Establishment and Central Landing School under the command of Sqn Ldr Louis Strange.

107

Its instructors were mainly RAF fabric workers with parachuting experience and members of the Army Physical Training Corps. When Sqn Ldr (later Grp Capt) Maurice Newnham became CO it was renamed the No.1 Parachute Training School and all the instructors were drawn from the RAF's Physical Fitness branch. Even today, paratroops are trained by the RAF Physical Education branch, and after several moves No.1 Parachute Training School still thrives – at Brize Norton (Oxon). During the war there were two other parachute training schools, in India and the Middle East. In 1940, prospective paratroops' introduction to training was a jump from a roof platform in No.6 or No.7 Hangar at the training centre, later wryly named 'Kilkenny's Circus' after the officer who devised the training schedule. The hangars were demolished in 1996 and replaced by a new British Airways terminal. When the trainees made practice drops from aircraft over Tatton Park, a few miles to the south-west, they did so emerging from the dark wombs of half a dozen cumbersome, cramped, smelly, modified Whitley bombers. The first air jumps at Tatton Park were made by the pull-off method, soon abandoned, from a platform at the rear of the plane; others were made through apertures in the floor.

For 135 descents, using the standard Irvin 28ft (8.5m) flat diameter trainer parachute (the RAF emergency version was 24ft (7.3m), there were no serious mishaps. The ripcord had been adapted for automatic deployment by static line, one end of which was hooked to a cable inside the aircraft, the other to a breaker cord, then to the ripcord on the jumper's pack. But the 136th jump, by a Royal Army Service Corps driver, was fatal. His parachute failed to open and he died instantly. The next day, with 200lb (91kg) dummies attached, three more parachutes failed. Jumping stopped for five days while a solution was sought. Raymond Quilter, of the GQ Parachute Company, came up with the idea of substituting rigging-lines-first deployment for the traditional canopy-first, so that the parachute would open well clear of the plane. Quilter retained the Irvin canopy and harness, but redesigned the packing system. The canopy was stowed in a bag attached by static line to the aircraft, but the rigging lines were packed on a flap over the mouth of the bag. This method, incorporated into the famous X-type parachute for paratroops, and later the 'statichute' which used a static line, was to earn Quilter a government award of £27,500 after the war.

Any apprehension generated by parachute training was compounded by the unpopularity, unsuitability and danger of jumping from the standard Whitley bomber. Pressure brought to bear on the

Air Ministry to bring in the more suitable Bristol Bombay fell on deaf ears. 'If you don't like the Whitley,' the Ministry said in effect, 'then don't have paratroops.' The War Office surrendered, and the Whitleys were retained. Until the introduction of the Dakota with side exits for jumpers later in the war, the Whitley and the similarly unpopular Wellington remained in use. Holes in the floor, rather like funnels which narrowed towards the bottom, took an unofficial toll of bloody casualties in plenty, as trainees smashed their faces on the sides in what became known grimly as the 'Whitley kiss'. Maintaining use of the unhappy Whitley revealed official stupidity at its worst. It damaged morale at a time when self-confidence was needed above all to inspire a new and untried force.

In September 1940, 342 officers and men of the newly formed irregulars called Commandos, which were intended to function as independent units, were recruited for parachute training. No fewer than thirty jibbed at the jump through the floor as the red warning light flicked to green. Twenty were injured or found unsuitable, and two were killed through parachute failure – in those days there were no reserve parachutes. Soon afterwards, Commando paratroops carried out Britain's first airborne raid, on the Apulia aqueduct in southern Italy. Through no fault of theirs it was not a success, because a crucial pier turned out to be made of reinforced concrete instead of the expected stone, and so failed to give way to their quarter ton of explosives. What did give way was the Italians' sang-froid; they were amazed at the audacity of the raid. More productive by far was the paratroops' raid on Bruneval, near Le Havre, where in February 1942 a combined force attacked a radiolocation (radar) station and escaped with vital pieces of equipment, data and several prisoners to gunboats waiting offshore.

Casualties in the field were expected and inevitable, but in training, theoretically avoidable. In fact, at first injuries and worse were disconcertingly high at Ringway. To win their paratrooper's wings, recruits had to make a controlled jump from a tower, two jumps from a captive balloon (much disliked because of the sensation it gave of height), and five more from aircraft. But of 543 men who underwent the two-week course at Ringway towards the end of 1941, thirty-eight received serious injury, including fractured spines and broken legs. Three months later, forty-eight out of 238 on a similar course were injured and two men killed. Investigations established a mysterious tendency for parachute rigging lines to twist, thus delaying the canopy's deployment. Each parachute was equipped with four lift-webs – strips of webbing extending upwards about three feet to where the rigging lines sprang from rings up to the canopy – and these gave a measure of control and steerability when pulled. When the lines twisted, this was impossible and the parachute drifted helplessly. With each serious injury, suggestions of providing a reserve parachute were renewed but rejected on the grounds of cost and weight; the main parachute already weighed 25lb (10kg), it was argued. Grp Capt Newnham, the CO, offered a solution. He devised a new method of packing the rigging lines so that their loops sat vertically, each loop enclosed in its own canvas pocket to eliminate risk of entanglement. Leslie Irvin was strongly in favour of this modification; so was Air Marshal Trafford Leigh-Mallory, C-in-C Fighter Command, who convened a conference to discuss parachuting equipment. The discussion came to an abrupt end, however, when a member of an Air Ministry directorate, fresh from operational duties at his Whitehall desk, announced that his department was quite satisfied with progress already being made. So nothing more was heard of Newnham's idea; equipment remained as it was.

Among the thousands to be trained as parachutists were agents to be dropped by Special Operations Executive into occupied Europe. More than 1,300 members of the gallant French section alone passed through Ringway. None of them was injured during training, but six were killed during their drops into France. In one case the plane went in too low; one man landed badly, two were killed through faulty parachutes, one because he forgot to hook up his static line in the aircraft, and another died for reasons unknown. Agents were able to take some equipment down with them. The lift-webs on their harness were made specially long so that radios and other items could be hung there during the descent. A continual flow of supplies was maintained to agents in the field; in total, about 120,000 shock-resisting package containers were parachuted into France. Packers became so expert that even 200 bottles of printing ink, destined for an underground newspaper, arrived without a single casualty.

Much care was of course taken in packing man-carrying parachutes. Each one took about twenty-five minutes to fold, stow and be inspected. To avoid the effects of damp and casing, packers had to remove an unused parachute from its pack after two months. And it could not be used for more than twenty-five descents. Packing was the preserve of the Women's Auxiliary Air Force, the WAAFs. (Women are now an integral part of the RAF.)

Packer and repairer were recognised trades for those aged between seventeen and forty-three, and there were about 2,800 of them throughout the country. One of their routine tasks was tracking the career of each parachute in a record book so that it could not be overworked or escape repair. Over Tatton Park, parachute drops became safer. The odds against a fatal one lengthened from one in 6,000 in 1942 to one in 100,000 in three years. Accidents were due to bad jumping or faulty equipment rather than careless packing. Signs above the packers' heads were a constant reminder of their responsibility – 'A man's life depends on every parachute you pack' – and despite the tedious succession of jokes from parachutists about being able to draw a second parachute if the first failed to work, they treated their task with dedicated seriousness. For thirty-two years, confessed one padre after his first jump from a training balloon, his whole trust had reposed in God; but for a few seconds, until his parachute opened, his confidence was transferred to a WAAF parachute packer. Not without good cause: by 1945, well over 400,000 descents had been made by 60,000 paratroops passing through No.1 Parachute Training School, but only one fatal accident could ever be traced to faulty packing. The girls brought feminine sensitivity to their work, which helped to sustain the men who donned the parachutes. One of the Ringway packers, G. D. Martineau, crystallised her feelings with a moving little poem, which Hilary St John Saunders quoted in *The Red Beret*, the first and last verses of which ran:

> When they posted me here to the section,
> I was free as the pitiless air,
> Unashamed of confessed imperfection,
> Having no sort of burden to bear;
> I was not an incurable slacker;
> Neat, not fussy – I fancied of old;
> But today I'm a parachute packer,
> And my heart takes a turn with each fold . . .
>
> So is conscience awakened and care born
> In the heart of a negligent maid.
> Aeolus, fight for the Airborne,
> Whom I strive with frail fingers to aid.
> Give my heroes kind wind and fair weather,
> Let no parachute sidle or slump.
> For today we go warring together,
> And my soul will be there at the jump.

In many lands did the men of the Parachute Regiment, and the thoughts of those at home, take wing and go 'warring together'. Given their proudly borne sobriquet, the 'Red Devils', by grudging German admirers in North Africa in 1942, they fought with immense panache and distinction, sometimes against hopeless odds, on many fronts and often on no cohesive front at all. But in terms of numbers, none of their actions compared with the scale of the German invasion of Crete in 1941, the first occasion in history on which an island was captured from the air. It was just as well. Though Crete fell in eleven days, the cost of the German victory was too high for Hitler. Of 25,000 German troops landed by parachute and glider and from the sea, well over 4,000 were killed and 2,000 wounded; and 170 out of 600 transport aircraft were destroyed. Never again did the Führer try an attack on this scale, and plans to invade Malta using paratroops were abandoned.

Unlike the Allies, Germany, though originally in the van of paratroop warfare, never fully appreciated its strategic value. Consequently, the German *Fallschirmjäger*, formed in the mid-1930s from volunteers and regarded as the flower of German soldierhood, were rarely used as airborne troops after the Crete invasion. 'Crete has shown that the day of the paratrooper is over,' Hitler ruefully told his paratroop commander, General Kurt Student of the 11th Air Corps. At their formation, the *Fallschirmjäger* numbered about 1,000; at the end of the war there were 250,000, but now performing the more mundane role of élite infantrymen. The first parachute used by German paratroops, the RZ1, was unsatisfactory in that it gave the jumper a severe shock when opening. To lessen this, the Germans took to making spread-eagled dives when they left the plane. Nor did the RZI always fully open, and too many landings were made too fast. In 1940, this parachute gave way to the RZ16 which, though a sound parachute, lacked the quick-release device provided on later models. Like the British man-carrying parachute, the German version, made of silk, artificial silk or Perlon, was camouflaged. But the German paratroops protested because they thought the dyes made the canopies less likely to develop and slowed them down when they did. This notion was quite baseless, but they were not satisfied until the German High Command ordered that all camouflaged parachutes should be dusted with French chalk before packing.

Although the role of German paratroops diminished after Crete, that of their British counterparts expanded. They fought with distinction in North Africa, Italy, Sicily, during the invasion of France, and at the Rhine crossing. On 17 September 1944 began the airborne assault at Arnhem in which, although British paratroops earned their own brand of glory behind enemy lines, endowing themselves with an aura surviving long into posterity, three quarters of the 10,000 who took part were killed, wounded or missing. This was due as much to a series of errors of judgement, bad planning and under-estimating the strength of enemy opposition as from the opposition itself. But whatever faults there were could hardly be laid at the door of the Red Devils. To the peoples of occupied Europe, imprisoned in their homelands, the descending paratroops were more like angels, striking a blow towards their deliverance.

And there were other 'angels' in this army. Many recruits, objecting to participating in war on principle, had a tougher war than most with the Royal Army Medical Corps or Non-Combatant Corps, having been attached to paratroop units with the Parachute Field Ambulance. They were usually equipped with revolvers, but only for self-defence and the protection of the wounded, though some refused even to carry these and landed on D-Day completely unarmed. The Parachute Field Ambulance dropped on to the battlefield with the main attacking force, bringing down with them canisters of medical supplies. Immediately once they had landed they set up field surgical and dressing stations. Surgeons who officered these units often carried out serious operations with the enemy only yards away. The axiomatic toughness of paratroops concealed a compassion for the wounded whichever side these were on. During the Sicily invasion, a friend of mine, the late Eric Stevens – a staff sergeant in the Parachute Field Ambulance and a non-combatant volunteer – was cycling with a message to headquarters when he spotted a German soldier lying by the roadside, seriously wounded and obviously near death. Stevens stopped, crossed the road, gave the German a shot of morphine, and returned to his bicycle – only to be immediately hit by an enemy mortar shell. Despite this, he went on to rescue some of his wounded British comrades under fire. He was awarded the Military Medal.

There was high mutual respect between friend and foe. R. M. Wingfield, in *The Only Way Out*, pays tribute to the German para-troops for whom, he says, 'we felt quite a professional affection'. They fought cleanly, he says, and treated prisoners with the respect they expected from the British. He tells the touching story of an incident in which two German stretcher-bearers, seeing one of a couple of their British counterparts injured by a mortar bomb while treating a casualty, went out themselves into no-man's land and carried the injured British stretcher-bearer, under the direction of their compatriot, to the British lines. 'Waving farewell, they doubled back to the wood. We cheered them all the way back. A twelve-hour truce followed. No one had the heart to spoil this gesture by firing. So, temporarily, the war stopped. Next morning they were gone.'

Besides dropping British soldiers in this increasingly mobile war, the parachute was used for supply-dropping on a spectacular scale. In some theatres of war, such as Burma, it was often the only means of conveying supplies to armies thrust deep into enemy territory where landing aircraft was impossible. 'The vulnerable artery is the line of communication winding through the jungle,' said Chindit leader Maj-Gen Orde Wingate. 'Have no line of communication on the jungle floor. Bring in the goods, like Father Christmas, down the chimney.' In 1943 a vast number of parachutes for air supply was needed, not only for the Chindits but also for the main body of the 14th Army, poised to attack. Then came bad news for its commander, Lt-Gen (later Field Marshal) William Slim. Supplies of parachutes from India would be far below their needs, and because there was a worldwide parachute shortage, none would be forthcoming from Britain either. Slim had two options. He could either trim his plans or seek some alternative to parachute silk. First he thought of using paper, as the Germans had, but the paper being made in Calcutta was the wrong sort. So he settled for jute, and with the co-operation of Calcutta businessmen, who showed a generous lack of interest in payment, the 'parajute' was a reality within a month. It compensated for lack of porosity by having several smaller vents all over the canopy, rather than a large one in the apex. And, remarkably, it was only about one seventh less efficient than the standard silk version. The parajutes, which cost about a pound each to make compared with twenty times that for the standard parachute, were intended for supply-dropping in the Burma campaign. Slim's reward for using his imagination in time of dire need was admonishment from higher authority for failing to order parachutes through the proper channels!

When the war began, in 1939, there had been little call for supplies to be dropped from the air. Britain's biggest container was made to take only 150lb (68kg) of supplies, and its parent parachute was only 14ft (4.2m) flat diameter. But as the airborne army built up, so did the means of delivery. On D-Day, the RAF was dropping jeeps and anti-tank guns weighing 1½ tons (1,524kg) each, borne on clusters of three or four parachutes 60ft (18m) in diameter to maintain stability. The large parachutes were difficult to maintain in the field. Almost as the war ended, a 42ft (12.8m) parachute with shaped gores instead of straight-sided ones was replacing the 60ft (18m) version. Clusters of these could be released safely at aircraft speeds of up to 200mph (324kph). Originally, heavy loads were dropped using the static-line system employed by paratroops. It was first tried when dropping an airborne lifeboat on a triple cluster of 32ft (9.6m) parachutes, but because this damaged the aircraft a new method of release was developed. First, a small auxiliary parachute (like an ordinary one but with several vanes running up the centre) would emerge, and this would pull out a 12ft (3.6m) retarder parachute, which had two different fabric porosities in the canopy and was designed to open suddenly. Below the retarder were the main parachute packs, from which the canopies would be hauled out by the weight of the fast-falling lifeboat. Containers to accompany paratroops were dropped from the bomb bays of aircraft. Ideally, they had to go down in the middle of a 'stick' of men, so as to be quickly on hand at ground level. To prevent it fouling paratroops' parachutes, a delay mechanism was introduced: a spring-loaded metal arm which could be adjusted to allow opening after between a half a second and six seconds. The container, with its parachute coloured for easy identification, would then fall below the stick of parachutists and open without endangering them.

The Germans, not satisfied with containers merely for supplies, dreamed up an advanced version for men – a 'human bomb'. Four parachutes supported the container, which was 9ft (2.7m) long and 6ft (1.8m) in diameter, with three saboteurs inside, complete with weapons. Once on terra firma, the men would carry out their task, return and lock themselves inside the containers and lie waiting for a low-flying aircraft to sweep in and hook them aloft without landing. The parachute was also the vehicle carrying the first of Hitler's 'secret weapons', the non-contact magnetic or acoustic sea-mine, which began to take its toll of Allied shipping only a few days after the war began. German planes dropped these parachute mines in the Thames and Humber estuaries, and Harwich harbour on 21 November 1939. The following night, more were dropped at Shoeburyness and one was captured intact and dismantled to disclose 660lb (299kg) of explosive. The British also dropped their magnetic mines by parachute – the jute hessian type. The mines were cylindrical and blunt-ended rather than streamlined, because they did not need to fall at speed. The whole object of the parachute was to ensure a soft landing so that the mine's sensitive delayed-action mechanism was undamaged.

German 'land mines', which were actually naval parachute mines that exploded on contact, having descended in deadly silence, were for a time the most feared means of destruction in air raids on London. The parachute's slow descent ensured that a mine exploded on the surface of the ground, causing maximum damage. No one who has seen the results of a 'land mine' explosion is likely to forget it. Many, however, failed to explode, thus dislocating the ARP (Air Raid Precautions) and other services, to whom they came as an unpleasant surprise. On one occasion an unexploded mine stopped fireboats from reaching blitz-torn London – above Tower Bridge. Another, dropped in April 1941, put the entire east end of St Paul's Cathedral in jeopardy, until dealt with by a Royal Navy bomb disposal squad. Meanwhile, the Germans used parachutes to recover, out over the Baltic, practice A-5 rockets. These were the precursors of the German V2, the worst of Hitler's secret weapons, of which 1,115 were to rain down on a hapless London – and which the Führer mistakenly believed would crucially demoralise the British and force a surrender.

Reconnaissance flares were dropped by the British over German territory on cotton parachutes. Although used throughout the war, they did not always open satisfactorily, and were of little value because they fell too quickly. They were designed before the war, and thus before high-speed aircraft were brought into service and before the importance of canopy fabrics was fully understood. Because it was too late to amend the design, the war ended with an inadequate product. For anti-submarine attacks, the British used a slow-falling parachute flare which dropped at about six feet per second, or about a third of the speed of a paratroop descent. Para*sheets*, which acted like parachutes but were formed of strips of fabric rather than gores, were used for these. To economise on silk they were of a man-made fibre called Celanese Fortisan which occupied little space when folded. To increase stability, a pair of parasheets were used for each flare.

Among Britain's unsung weapons was a cleverly contrived device called PAC – the parachute-and-cable rocket – which was used to defend airfields and ports in England. Marauding German planes, zooming in for low-level attacks, suddenly found steel cables snaking up 500ft (152m) into the sky ahead of them, with a parachute at the top to keep the cable in the air long enough to ward off danger. The PAC was adapted by the Royal Navy's Directorate of Miscellaneous Weapon Development for use at sea and designed by a company which normally made marine rockets for saving life. After much experimentation with linen and nylon cord supplied by a West End store, the team produced a strong canopy and rigging lines. Soon merchant ships were equipped with PAC, and in 1941 reports filtered through giving evidence of its value. The small convoy vessel *Fireglow*, for example, was caught in a big air attack when the mate, standing by one of its PAC guns, suddenly yanked the firing lanyard and up shot the cable, neatly slicing the wing off a German bomber. Soon enemy pilots were taking home worrying stories about the mysterious and lethal 'spirals', as they called them, which kept appearing from nowhere. When the PAC left the secret list in 1943, it was known to have brought down nine German planes and saved at least thirty-five Allied ships from bombing attacks.

Chapter Twelve

By a Silken Thread

B ritain's bombing offensive in the first part of World War II was disappointingly wasteful and woefully inadequate, according to figures quoted in at least two reports in 1941. RAF bombs, said Prime Minister Winston Churchill, were being dropped with only twenty-five per cent accuracy, and a study of aerial photography in August that year showed that only a third of RAF crews credited with successful attacks had bombed within five miles of their targets. Later, thanks to the Halifaxes, Lancasters and Mosquitos of the RAF's Pathfinder Force, formed in 1942 and equipped with new navigational aids, raids on Germany became remarkably successful. To this, the parachute made a valuable contribution.

The Pathfinders were an élite corps assembled and commanded throughout their three-year life by a brilliant navigator and former Imperial Airways pilot, Grp Capt (later Air Vice-Marshal) Donald Bennett. Their purpose was to lead and light the way for Allied bombers over enemy territory and signpost their dropping points. There was much opposition to the Force initially, not least from Bomber Command's C-in-C, Air Marshal Arthur Harris, who disliked the prospect of having to cream off some of the best air crews to form it. Years later, with the benefit of hindsight, Bennett was to insist, perhaps extravagantly, that the Pathfinder concept was 'the greatest single factor in victory', making way as it did for repeated stabs at Germany's industrial heart. When the war began, magnesium parachute flares were found to be unreliable. Their inaccuracy was due largely to time-fusing rarely being properly adjusted; nor did aircraft ever seem to be at the planned height. And the back-glare from the flares was so strong as to dazzle aircrews, thus nullifying any advantage from illumination of the ground. On the formation of the Pathfinders, Bennett counteracted the glare, installing an umbrella-like hood between the flare and the main canopy of the parachute. Because the height of release had to be flexible and match varying conditions, he abandoned the time-governed release fuse and substituted a barometric device so that the parachute opened at a pre-selected height. The flare was used to light up targets on the ground, and it was followed down by the target indicator (TI), a collection of Roman candles which exploded two or three hundred feet (60 to 120m) above the ground and continued its display after landing.

The parachute flare was especially valuable in sky-marking, when cloud was too dense for bomb aimers to see target indicators on the ground, though many of Bennett's colleagues scoffed until they saw the results. Dropped above the cloud according to readings from the Pathfinders' navigational radar devices, H2S or Oboe, the flare would burn in varying colours depending on the code chosen for the day or the particular operation. It burned for four minutes and was dropped in such a position as to be accurately placed after three minutes of drift. Bomb aimers would drop their loads the moment the flare entered their sights – in theory, exactly on target. This tactic, employed throughout the latter part of the war, figured in the highly successful attack on Essen on 9 January 1943 which was made through thick cloud. It was obvious to the Germans that blind bombing was being used, but Hitler could hardly bring himself to believe it. So angered was he, according to Bennett, that he threatened some of his intelligence advisers with execution. The parachute flare was in brave hands indeed. Between the time the Pathfinders were formed and the end of the war they had flown more than 50,000 individual sorties against 3,440 targets. Their planes were often unarmed, and crews were required to make a tour of sixty operational sorties against the bomber crews' normal thirty. It is hardly surprising that 3,600 Pathfinders were killed in action – about one in thirteen of Bomber Command's entire aircrew losses.

For Bennett, the parachute proved doubly useful: not only did it contribute to the achievements of his Pathfinder Force, it also saved his life. Bennett was commanding a squadron of Halifaxes on a mission bombing the German warship *Tirpitz* near Trondheim in Norway. The object was to drop five 1,000lb (450kg) spherical mines down the banks of the fjord and explode them against the ship's hull under water. Bennett's aircraft came in for the bombing run at only 200ft (61m), but was badly hit by anti-aircraft fire. The crew kept it on course, but when they arrived over the ship's presumed location they cursed their luck: it was hidden beneath an artificial camouflage 'fog'. The Halifax, a starboard engine blazing fiercely, turned to make another run. It released the mines as accurately as it could, then tackled the next obstacle, one which was literally almost insuperable. For ahead of them soared a 3,000ft (915m) mountain range, and both the plane's starboard engines were now burning. Bennett, realising he was certain to crash, throttled the outer port engine in an effort to stabilise, and gave the order to abandon aircraft. At this point, to his horror, he suddenly became aware that he alone was without a parachute, which was stowed away down the fuselage. Fortunately Colgan, his flight engineer, found it for him and clipped it on to the quick connector snap-hooks on his chest. (This was the usual method of parachute attachment for bomber crews, who needed their hands free and had to be able to move about the plane unencumbered; fighter pilots wore seat-packs which they sat on like cushions in their cockpits.) The Halifax was losing height so rapidly that there was hardly time to escape. Bennett leapt through the hatch, pulled the ripcord and the parachute opened a few moments before he hit the snow. He and his colleagues dodged the Germans and eventually reached home via Sweden.

Thus another member was recruited to the Caterpillar Club. Since the club's inauguration in 1922 there have been more than 32,000 in the European branch alone, most having qualified for membership during World War II. Irvin himself, however, never qualified as a 'caterpillar' because, although during his lifetime he made more than 300 parachute descents, he never had to make one in an emergency – a pre-condition for club membership. War came, and with it a brisk demand for parachutes, bringing prosperity to Irvin and his factory in Letchworth (Herts) where he remained practically throughout the war, even though he was an American citizen. Irvin developed a fierce vicarious patriotism on behalf of his adoptive country. He would travel round Letchworth using a bicycle and not a car, ostensibly to save petrol, and would give frequent pep-talks to his factory employees over the loudspeaker system, urging that every possible minute should be devoted to the war effort in general and parachute production in particular. He also enjoyed long talks with his staff, and would throw a party or give a cowboy film show on the flimsiest pretext. He had a rare flair for the public relations coup. One day, when he heard that several American airmen had baled out in the vicinity of Letchworth, Irvin sent a car post-haste to collect them. Within the hour, while still trembling from the shock of the jump, the airmen found themselves faced with another ordeal – making a morale-boosting appearance on stage in the factory and saying a few encouraging words to the workers.

Irvin had started out in the United States as a circus performer, and never lost his showbusiness skill. Grp Capt Maurice Newnham, commanding officer of paratroop training at Ringway, would recall Irvin's visits to Ringway and his favourite parlour trick: standing on his head against a piano playing 'I want to be Happy' and drinking a glass of beer, all at the same time. One of Irvin's 'caterpillars' had an escape record that eclipsed even Lindbergh's four escapes in the 1920s. The young RAF fighter pilot Tony Woods-Scawen managed to avoid disaster eleven times, with four forced landings, three crash-landings and four parachute jumps. His first escape, which gained him membership of the Caterpillar Club, was in June 1940 when his Hurricane was shot down over Dieppe. Presumed missing, he turned up eight days later at Tangmere airfield (West Sussex) with the parachute that had saved him. He had slipped through from behind the German lines and joined a British Expeditionary Force unit evacuating from France in the Dunkirk withdrawal. He made three more parachute escapes, but his fifth jump was made when his plane was too low, and he hit the ground and was killed before the parachute had time to develop.

The annals of the Caterpillar Club, whose members are entitled to wear a little gold caterpillar brooch, are filled with stories of exciting escapes, many by the narrowest of margins. In the 1930s Ernst Udet, the German fighter ace who parachuted down after a dogfight in World War I, became an Irvin 'caterpillar'. In July 1934 the tail of his Curtiss Hawk broke off during dive-bombing practice over Berlin's Tempelhof airport. His parachute opened just in time, with only feet to spare. Six years later, as a high-ranking Luftwaffe officer under Goering in World War II, Udet was helping to make 'caterpillars' of British aircrews. One of the unluckiest of these was Flt Lt James Nicolson, a Hurricane pilot of 249 Squadron who, on a cloudless afternoon in August 1940, qualified for Fighter Command's only VC of the war. Nicolson had never had the opportunity of getting a shot at a German before, so when a group of Junkers 88s droned into the Gosport area he welcomed the chance of making his first kill. As he and his flight flew in, however, Nicolson was dismayed to see a squadron of Spitfires move in and shoot down all the Junkers before his own Hurricanes could get within range. Turning back disappointed, Nicolson suddenly found himself attacked by a Messerschmitt.

Cannon shells ripped through his plane, and splinters injured his left eye and left foot. Flames leapt up in the cockpit. Just as he was preparing to bale out, Nicolson spotted his attacker speeding past him. He sat back and decided to take his revenge. Ignoring his own plight, he dived down after the German, firing rounds by the score until it crashed. By this time his hands were badly burnt, his instrument panel smashed and melting from the heat. Desperately, he heaved himself away from the remains of his charred seat belt and threw himself out. Luckily, his parachute was undamaged and opened safely. He sailed earthwards, bleeding profusely from his wounds, only to be shot in the legs by a Civil Defence worker. He survived this and flew again to win the DFC, but was killed in an air crash in the Far East at the end of the war.

Twice the parachute came to the aid of the legless fighter pilot, Grp Capt (later Sir) Douglas Bader. He had lost both legs well before the war in a flying accident in 1931, and had been invalided out of the RAF. But he fought a determined and ultimately successful campaign with the authorities to rejoin, and became a squadron leader and a leading figure in the Battle of Britain and promoter of the famous, and controversial, 'big wing' policy. According to his biographer Paul Brickhill (author of *Reach for the Sky*), Bader was the best fighter leader and tactician throughout the air war, and among the best pilots. Bader qualified as a member of the Caterpillar Club on 9 August 1941 when he was a wing commander and taking part in a fighter sweep over northern France. (This, incidentally, was two months after the strangest parachutist of the war, Hitler's deputy Rudolf Hess, dropped from his plane over Scotland on an alleged peace-seeking mission.) Shortly after Bader's Spitfire had crossed the coast, a Messerschmitt 109 intercepted at 24,000ft (7,320m) and attacked. In the ensuing dogfight, Bader suddenly saw chunks flying off his plane, and as he glanced round saw his tail unit had practically disappeared. As its nose went down, the Spitfire went into a vertical dive and began to spin. Bader knew there was only one way out now – baling out, if he could. He heaved himself up with his hands, got his artificial leg outside the plane, and hauled on the other. Nothing happened; it was firmly lodged in the cockpit. Then suddenly the leather straps snapped and Bader shot out of the plane, leaving his right leg where it was. The Spitfire had dropped through the sky for 20,000ft (6,100m) over Béthune in northern France before Bader's parachute opened. He made a painful landing on his remaining artificial leg, which the impact pushed up into his chest. He was captured by the Germans and taken to St Omer hospital. When the doctors saw what was left of his legs, they had no need to ask his name, for to the Germans Bader was almost as legendary as he was among his own countrymen. When Bader asked for the missing leg to be reclaimed from the wrecked Spitfire, the Germans not only rescued it but made a brilliant job of repairing it. Meanwhile, with Goering's permission, they also radioed the British to send a spare. This the Germans wanted landed by Lysander, which they promised to guarantee free passage. They would allow a British fighter escort to the French coast, and Messerschmitts would then take over. That was the plan, but the British would have none of it. Dismissing the German offer as a propaganda ploy, they chose to drop the leg by parachute from a Blenheim sent over on a normal bombing raid. Meanwhile, Bader was anything but a model prisoner; he saw it as his duty not to be one, but to be as difficult and obstructive as he could. It was shortly after his recapture following the first of his attempted escapes that his RAF comrades at Tangmere kept their appointment. As the British planes streaked home from a bombing raid, they flew over St Omer airfield leaving a long yellow box to float down by parachute. It was addressed to the commandant and contained Bader's spare right leg. At the end of the war in Europe, Bader, now with a double DSO and double DFC and with the rank of group captain, led his fighter pilots in triumph once more across the southern skies in the first Battle of Britain fly-past on 15 September 1945.

In the annals of flight, one of the most incredible exploits involving any escaping airman was the jump of a Lancaster rear gunner, Flt Sgt Nicholas Alkemade, who miraculously survived a desperate leap from his crippled plane at 18,000ft (5,490m) over Germany without a parachute at all. It happened on the night of 24 March 1944 when Alkemade, veteran of a dozen night raids over Berlin, climbed into his lonely gun turret and joined yet another 300-bomber raid. The outward flight was uneventful, and after dropping its 4,000lb (1,814kg) blockbuster bomb and a host of incendiaries in what seemed a remarkably trouble-free trip, the Lancaster turned for home. Then, suddenly, a roaming Junkers 88 attacked the Lancaster, coming from the rear and shattering Alkemade's gun turret. Alkemade replied with his Brownings, and after long bursts saw the Junkers plunge down, fatally crippled. His satisfaction at this was short-lived, though, for meanwhile the rest of the Lancaster had become a mass of flames which poured along the fuselage, cutting the rear gunner off completely from his parachute stowage. Alkemade now faced exactly the dilemma of parachute-less aircrews in World War I: remain with the plane or jump, with death an each-way certainty? Alkemade jumped. By all natural laws he should have died, his body smashed like Robert Cocking's from his ill-fated cone-shaped parachute a century earlier. But no. Ninety seconds later, stunned, bleeding, burned but alive, Alkemade crashed through the branches of a pine forest and hit a bank of snow. When the Germans found him, they did not believe his story. But why should they? It simply defied belief; it must be a trick. How could a man fall three and a half miles and live? Only when they realised that the webbing straps on part of his parachute harness were still folded and tied down, and when they retrieved his ripcord and cable from the wrecked Lancaster twenty miles away, did they accept the truth. Alkemade did not expect the feting staged by the Germans; he was content just to be alive. But for posterity, they drew up a handwritten certificate to corroborate his story, which was signed by a British Flight Lieutenant and two Flight Sergeants in the prison camp. Alkemade died in 1987, after Providence had lent him forty-three extra years of life. Thus he had proved what until his leap in 1944 was an untenable proposition: that to make a safe bale-out, a parachute is not strictly necessary. But it helps.

However, during World War II even escaping *with* a parachute was no guarantee of safety. Aircrew could be, as indeed some were, shot as they made emergency drops on parachutes, though this was forbidden under a draft code drawn up by the Commission of Jurists at The Hague in 1923. Britain had not accepted this code, though she generally observed the rule. Germany, however, did not. In 1941 Sir Samuel Hoare, the Air Secretary, revealed that attacks had been made on twelve British pilots leaving four of them dead. One authenticated case in 1940 was of a Hurricane pilot who was killed in this way over south-east England. He had baled out at 15,000ft (4,575m). An Air Ministry Bulletin reported: 'As he was floating down, three Messerschmitts swooped on him and opened fire on his swaying figure. He was riddled with bullets.' On the other hand, there were those who were more chivalrous. A Hurricane pilot who ultimately landed in a cucumber frame in southern England reported in another Bulletin: 'As I floated down, one of the Messerschmitts appeared. The pilot circled around me and I was alarmed ... I felt very much that he would shoot me. And I felt helpless. But he didn't shoot. He behaved very well. He

124

flew so near, the noise of his aircraft was terrific. He flew around me about one and a half times and then suddenly opened a piece of his hood and waved to me. Then he dived towards the sea and made off across the Channel to France. I'd like to know why he let me get away. He could have got me as simply as anything. But he didn't even try.' This was a highly unofficial gesture, because just before the fall of France in 1940 Nazi Germany had the audacity to complain that their pilots were being fired on by the French. This could have been accidental, of course; the French were at that time on the *qui vive* for enemy paratroops, not escaping pilots. Nevertheless, Goering threatened to kill fifty French prisoners for every German pilot shot in this way. The Italians showed particular callousness towards Allied aircrews in North Africa. In 1943, one Italian newspaper even urged that aiming at them as they parachuted down would make good target practice for anti-aircraft gunners.

In World War II there was a risk, admittedly a small one, of attack once a baled-out airman had been taken prisoner. Under a decree issued by Hitler in 1942 some Allied Commandos and paratroops were executed in captivity, in contravention of the rules of war protecting prisoners. When the bombing of Germany was stepped up in 1943, civilians were actively encouraged to lynch airmen escaping by parachute. Public admission of the Axis's guilt in this respect came during the Nuremberg trials in 1946. Walter Schellenberg, deputy to German security chief Ernst Kaltenbrunner, alleged that he heard Kaltenbrunner say: 'All officers of the SD [*Sicherheitsdienst*, the Nazi intelligence and security body] and Security Police are to be informed that pogroms of the populace against English and American terror-flyers are not to be interfered with. On the contrary, this hostile mood is to be encouraged.' International law makes it quite clear who among those descending on parachutes from aircraft is and is not entitled to protection. In 1977, the Additional Protocol I to the Geneva Conventions of 1949 (strangely not ratified by the UK) maintained provisions under the earlier draft 1923 Hague Rules, and is in force today. Article 42 of the API declares that 'no person parachuting from an aircraft in distress shall be made the object of attack during his descent'. On reaching the ground in territory controlled by an 'adverse Party', i.e. an enemy, 'they shall be given an opportunity to surrender before being made the object of attack, unless it is apparent that he is engaging in a hostile act'. That applies, for example, to aircrews. But it adds: '. . . Airborne troops are not protected by this Article.' Part of the

Manual of Military Law, which is to be included in a new *Tri-Service Manual of Armed Conflict Law* applying to the Army, Royal Navy and the RAF, states that 'it is lawful to fire on airborne troops and others engaged, or who appear to be engaged, on hostile missions whilst such persons are descending from aircraft, in particular over territory in control of the opposing forces, whether or not that aircraft has been disabled. It is, on the other hand, unlawful to fire at other persons descending by parachute from disabled aircraft.'

CHAPTER THIRTEEN

GOING WITH A BANG

As aircraft speeds began to edge upwards in the early 1930s, escape by parachute became a hazard in itself. Many pilots in some of the faster aircraft had to struggle with the blast from the airstream and a tendency to be forced back into their cockpits.

When No. 208 Squadron, Army Co-operation, RAF Egypt relinquished the 123mph (198kph) Bristol Fighter, a veteran from 1917, in favour of the 142mph (228kph) Armstrong Whitworth Atlas, which was capable of 200mph (322kph) in a power dive, Flg Off Peter Dudgeon believed emergency escapes from the new aircraft would be impossible. The pressure of the airstream, he feared, would wedge pilots in their cockpits. Dudgeon decided to try to counteract this danger. He acquired drawing instruments and a Meccano set, sketched plans and made a working model of his own invention, a kind of jack-in-a-box device that could save lives. His idea was to set the pilot's seat on a series of concentric sliding tubes with a powerful spring contained in each. They would be wound down on a key-operated ratchet and secured with a catch, which when released would immediately uncoil the springs and shoot both seat and pilot level with the top of the cockpit coaming. The pilot would then simply roll out and pull his parachute ripcord. Dudgeon sent a practical working model, with plans, via HQ Egypt to the Air Ministry, and waited hopefully. When they replied, they turned the idea down flat. The reason given was a cynical echo of that voiced against parachutes in World War I: any aid to escape would encourage pilots to save themselves rather than strive to bring their aircraft back to base. The captain, it appeared, must go down with his ship!

There is on record an ejection seat developed by Baron d'Odkolek and tested at Issy-les-Moulineaux in France. A dummy wearing a parachute was ejected by a small cannon from a plane in flight over Paris in 1912. What happened to this is obscure, but explosives would certainly be used for ejection a few decades on when high-speed aircraft would bring the problem of safe escape by parachute into high relief. In the late 1930s, Germany and Sweden had already made a start on designing and testing escape systems using compressed air and explosive cartridges for ejection seats. In January 1942 SAAB launched a test ejection using a dummy from a modified SAAB B17 – reportedly the first ejection from a modern aircraft – and in July 1943 the first aircraft with an ejection seat fired by an explosive charge, the SAAB 21, flew for the first time. By the end of July 1946 SAAB had ejected a pilot from a piston-engined SAAB J21 plane, also made in jet form. This was thought to be the first emergency ejection, but in fact the Germans had pre-empted SAAB more than four years earlier with an escape from a Heinkel. On 13 January 1942 Major Schenk was testing an experimental He 280 twin-engined fighter fitted with four pulse jets. It was equipped with a compressed air-operated ejection seat. Soon after take-off the plane ran into a snowstorm, and at nearly 7,900ft (2,410m) iced up. Realising the Heinkel was beyond his control, Schenk jettisoned his cockpit canopy, fired his ejection seat and saved his life, passing into history as the first person to make a successful emergency ejection.

The Germans had begun to experiment with 'catapult' seats as far back as 1938, fitting a Junkers 88 with compressed air devices the following year. Eventually these were installed on the Messerschmitt 262, Heinkel 219a-7 and 262a and Dornier 335A-6. The Germans' first production aircraft to be operational with an ejection seat as standard equipment was the Heinkel He 162, which used powder-charged ballistic catapult-type seats and went into service on 14 April 1945, a few weeks before the war ended. By the end of the war, about sixty Luftwaffe pilots and crew had made successful emergency ejections in action. Others were less fortunate. So powerful was the thrust of the compressed-air gun that spinal injuries became disturbingly frequent, and a thorough investigation into the limits of pilots' endurance and tolerance of impact was in progress even as Germany surrendered in 1945. Rather than risk further injuries to their own Servicemen, the Nazis fell back on other 'resources' – from their point of view, more expendable. In May 1945 members of the Institute of Aviation Medicine/Physiology Laboratory staffs who had been in Germany examining various research laboratories returned with reports, documents and information on Luftwaffe work in their field. These included details of experiments on the effect of air blast which the Nazis had conducted using 'volunteer' concentration camp inmates. The subjects were exposed with and without helmet and goggles protection for face and eyes. There were some dramatic pictures of exposed heads with cheeks and eyelids fluttering in air from a blower tunnel at reported speeds of up to 300 knots (346mph, 557kph).

In England, the problem of survival which for a time soured early jet flight was underlined in January 1944 when Sqn Ldr Douglas Davie, a Royal Aircraft Establishment test pilot, was killed at Farnborough. He was trying to escape from one of the new Gloster Meteor jet fighters when one of its twin engines exploded. Although he managed to climb from the cockpit, in the usual way over the side, he injured himself, lost consciousness in the tremendous blast of air and failed to pull his parachute ripcord. A few months later another pilot was killed testing a Meteor prototype at the Gloster works. Some kind of ejection seat was clearly needed, but just what the human body could tolerate in terms of violent acceleration was not known, and it was now to be studied by the RAF's Institute of Aviation Medicine. The parachute would still fulfil its traditional role, for the Air Staff had stipulated that mechanical ejection 'must utilise existing safety equipment'. Ejection seats came to be shaped round the parachute back pack, which fitted into a recess behind the airman. Experiments on a test rig at RAE, Farnborough using a 2,000ft (610m) long rocket track showed that a man could stand acceleration of up to twelve times the force of gravity, but not for longer than one tenth of a second. The RAE concluded that to meet requirements, including being thrown clear of a plane's tail, an ejection seat would have to blast the crew free at around 40ft (12m) per second.

Following the two fatal attempted Meteor escapes, the Air Staff invited James Martin, inventor, engineer and designer of four prototype aircraft – three of them advanced fighters – to try to find a practical solution to the problem of escape from high-speed aircraft. Martin, an Ulsterman, was energetic and had a lively, if volatile, inventive mind. He also had a deep interest in the use of explosives. Among his inventions early in the war was one to solve the problem of jammed cockpit hoods in Spitfires, which trapped forty pilots in their cockpits during the Battle of Britain. Martin devised a jettisonable canopy. All the pilot had to do was tug a small red rubber ball installed in the cockpit and dislodge retaining pins in the canopy, which was swept away in the slipstream. Another of Martin's inspired wheezes was an explosive-driven chisel, mounted in the leading edges of an aircraft's wings to cut the cables of barrage balloons. This was used to good effect against the Germans on raids over, for example, the well-defended Dortmund Ems Canal. He also invented a feed device for machine-gun ammunition belts. Martin seemed the ideal man to tackle the problem of escape from high-performance aircraft. He was to achieve world renown by using explosives not to destroy lives, but to save them, by turning men into human cannonballs attached to ejection seats, then landing them by parachute. His friend and partner, Capt Valentine Baker, crashed and was killed while testing a prototype aircraft in 1942, and although this tragedy was not the source of Martin's inspiration, he nevertheless had a personal as well as professional concern with air hazards.

The jet-engined Mark I Meteor was not the main source of pilots' and official concern over the dangers of emergency escape. At 445mph (716kph) maximum, this model was only a shade faster than existing piston-engined planes, but 600mph (966kph) models were in prospect. Initially, Martin was advised that any device he produced would be fitted to Spitfires and other high-performance aircraft forming the RAF's main fighter force. But in these planes, cockpit space was cramped, and the only workable device seemed to be a swinging arm set externally along the fuselage, fixed forward of the tail fin and reaching as far as the cockpit. The cockpit hood would be jettisoned and the spring-loaded arm, resembling a crane, would pluck the pilot up by his parachute harness, and the air flow would fling him clear. He would then pull his ripcord. The device impressed Sir Stafford Cripps, Minister of Aircraft Production, but it was decided – presumably because the Spitfire's day was almost over – not to put it into production. Another idea, soon abandoned, was a catapult operated by a sprung lever to throw a pilot out of the cockpit. Martin concentrated on devising a system of ejecting pilot and seat together, powered by a kind of gun. After making a model of an ejector, which the Air Ministry approved in principle, Martin was allocated a decrepit Boulton Paul Defiant fighter, an early and largely unsuccessful World War II plane crewed by a pilot and one turret gunner, and experiments with the 'bang seat' began.

Although James Martin was not the first in the ejection seat field, like Irvin with his ripcord parachute he quickly strode ahead and set up a commanding lead in technical development and adaptation which has never been overtaken. Today, more than fifty years later, Martin is honoured the world over as the father of the modern ejection seat. He got down to work in the autumn of 1944. He erected a test rig behind his factory at Higher Denham (Bucks), a 15ft (4.5m) high tripod, one of its legs resembling a children's playground slide, up which the ejection seat would be fired at high speed. A ratchet stop was provided to prevent the seat falling back uncontrollably. The rig was used to measure effects on the human body of increasingly severe accelerations. Medical experts were sceptical, but not the guinea-pig who cheerfully offered himself to make the first live test ride, a twenty-seven-year-old Irish experimental fitter named Benny Lynch. He first rode the rig on 24 January 1945, starting with shots to 4ft 8in (1.42m) and ending, after more powerful cartridges had been fitted into the seat, at 10ft (3m), alive and well but by all accounts not very comfortable.

The human spine, which with the pelvis would bear the brunt of the ejection seat's explosive system, soon claimed Martin's close attention. The spine is a closely integrated column of two dozen vertebrae, each cushioned by a cartilage disc and held together by ligaments and maintained vertical by muscles, with the head at the top and the spinal column secured in the pelvis at the bottom. It was the cartilage discs, acting as the vertebrae's shock absorbers, that were most at risk. They would have to sustain the most compression during the virtually instantaneous process of ejection. The Germans, with their use of compressed air, had greatly simplified ejection operation and reduced the initial acceleration. Using a cartridge was more efficient but gave an initial kick. The application of 'g' – upward acceleration – can be perfectly acceptable if it is not imposed too quickly. Martin conducted tests using dummies as well as human beings, and detailed measurements of 'g' loads and the amount of explosive required. One visiting reporter, Charles Andrews from *Aeroplane* magazine, had an unexpectedly unpleasant story to write when he volunteered for a live test. He rode the rig to a height of 10ft (3m), then complained of back pains and had to go into hospital suffering from crushed vertebrae. This injury prompted Martin to study high-speed film of the cartridge tests. He studied the composition of the human skeleton and watched hospital operations in order to learn more about the spine's construction, and managed to obtain a human backbone for his own use in mechanical tests. As a result, he rearranged the firing of the seat and by introducing a second cartridge – less powerful, and detonated by the first – achieved a smoother acceleration. He also redesigned the seat's footrests so that the spine's vertebrae would sit trim and square to each other. And he introduced a method using a quickly hauled-down face screen, or blind, to trigger the ejection gun. The face screen, made of canvas, was attached to a firing handle above the pilot's head, and when pulled downwards it would cover his face. It performed a double role: keeping the pilot sitting upright, and protecting his face from the deadly rush of air after the seat had been shot out of the aircraft. These improvements paid off. In no time, Bernard Lynch was able to experience a soft ride for 26ft 3in (8m) up a new 65ft (19.8m) test rig, and with no unpleasant side-effects.

On 11 May, three days after VE Day, Martin achieved his first ejection from a moving aircraft over England. The seat was loaded with bags of shot to represent the pilot, and it was caught in a net to conserve the equipment. The next day, at Wittering airfield (Cambs), he used a dummy and during the following weeks six more dummy ejections were made at Beaulieu (Hants) from the Defiant at speeds ranging up to 300mph (483kph). Martin was much encouraged by his successes using artificial cargo, but although he could calculate the degree of force needed to throw a pilot and his seat clear of a plane at various speeds, he did not know exactly how much upward compression thrust the human body could take without injury. Sqn Ldr (later Air Vice-Marshal) William Stewart, commandant of the Institute of Aviation Medicine, had described his experience of lying on his back on a horizontal rocket-fired trolley at Laffan's Plain, Farnborough, in which the shock of ejection was simulated by hydraulic rams. But more realistic tests were needed.

By 24 July 1946, Martin and his team felt they had solved enough problems to allow a live ejection from an aircraft. Benny Lynch, who insisted on packing his own parachute and was now a veteran of scores of test shots on the rig, was delighted to be the star performer once again. Official fears about the risks proved groundless. Flying at 320mph (515kph) in a Meteor 8,000ft (2,440m) above Chalgrove aerodrome near Benson (Oxon), Lynch hauled at the face-blind and blasted himself 25ft (7.6m) out into space. The seat worked, the back-pack parachute worked, and Lynch landed unhurt in the backyard of a public house. When the team found him he was calmly sipping a pint of beer in the saloon bar. A month later, he repeated the ejection at 420mph (676 kph) and from 12,000ft (3,660m). It was as successful as the first. Lynch made eighteen ejections during the seat's development, and on only one occasion was he injured – the last. He made a record ejection from 30,000ft, landed on a barbed-wire fence and broke an ankle. (Two years later he was awarded a much-deserved BEM for his valuable efforts as ejection seat 'guinea-pig', and eventually retired to Ireland.)

At one point in the test series, the pilot parachute, or drogue, gave trouble. At Beaulieu and Wittering the main parachute was released by a delayed-action device activated by a static line, which also unpinned the pack flaps so that a spring could shoot out the pilot drogue. The trouble was that the drogue's deployment tended to be affected by air turbulence round the seat after firing. Martin solved the problem by incorporating into the seat's design a gun and cartridge with the specific function of firing out the drogue.

Meanwhile, the US Navy had shown great interest in Martin's experiments, and after a demonstration ordered a 110ft (33.5m) test rig to be erected at Philadelphia. They also installed an ejection seat in the rear cockpit of a Douglas JD-1 aircraft. Eventually, on 1 November 1946, Lt Furtek made a live ejection using Martin-Baker equipment. The following year, the Air Ministry recognised Martin's years of development by adopting the Martin-Baker ejection seat and its Irvin emergency parachute as standard on all jet aircraft in the RAF and Royal Navy. This was a huge undertaking because aircraft already in service, such as the Meteor, Wyvern, Attacker, Sea Hawk and Venom, were obviously not designed to accommodate them. Apprehension from many official sources had to be dispelled; there were some pilots who regarded a cartridge under their cockpit seats as a potential hazard rather than the difference between life and death, and would have it removed. Much of the scepticism melted, however, when the 'bang seat' was seen to prove itself in an emergency. On 30 May 1949, John 'Jo' Lancaster, an Armstrong Whitworth test pilot, ejected at 5,000ft (1,515m) from a prototype AW-52 Flying Wing when it went out of control. Lancaster landed safely, apart from a few slight injuries, following what was in part a manual operation. After the seat left the aircraft, he had to unfasten his harness, thus discarding the seat, and pull the parachute ripcord – a method which made low-level escapes risky and often fatal if the parachute did not deploy in time. This one did – at 3,000ft (915m) – and Lancaster became the first ejection seat member of the Irvin Caterpillar Club.

By 1949 Martin was working on a fully automatic system which involved no more effort on the pilot's part than pulling the protective blind over his face, thus triggering off the whole ejection procedure. He also later improved his two-stage telescopic cartridge gun to give it an ejection velocity of 80ft (24.3m) per second. Tests with this, coupled with a time-release mechanism set at three seconds, proved that escapes could be made at low level if the aircraft was flying at least 119mph (191kph). When the time came for a live runway-level demonstration, Martin was forbidden, on grounds of risk, to use the Meteor he had been loaned. He went ahead anyway and received a congratulatory message from the Ministry when the test was successful. At Chalgrove airfield, on 3 September 1955, Sqn Ldr John Fifield ejected from the Meteor's rear cockpit during take-off, his parachute bearing him to earth in six seconds fully deployed, to the great satisfaction and relief of all, including himself. For this, Martin was personally thanked by the Air Minister. (A month earlier, twenty-two-year-old Flg Off Hedley Molland became the RAF's first pilot to eject at a speed faster than sound – from a Hawker Hunter in a steep dive at around 760mph (1,223kph). It was Martin's progress with low-level escapes that at last won him acceptance in the United States. Having shown active interest in his work in 1946, the US Navy had obtained ejection seats from American manufacturers for some years afterwards. But in 1957, following a ground-level demonstration by Flg Off Sidney Hughes at Patuxent River (Maryland), orders reached Britain for Martin-Baker ejection seats to be installed in eleven types of US naval aircraft.

Numerous improvements to the basic design of the ejection seat were made over the years, and many lives were being saved at a rescue rate of eighty-eight per cent. But it was the twelve per cent that worried Martin – a serious matter of twenty pilots a year killed, more than half of them for lack of height when leaving the plane, which itself had a high 'sink rate', i.e. descended rapidly. The solution was to give more height to the ejection seat's trajectory, to give time for the parachute to open but without increasing the strain on the airman. Martin had already reached the limit of performance with the ejection cartridge gun. Now he tried using rockets. By placing these under the seat and directing them through its centre of gravity, he could give the seat more height and, by reducing the power of the cartridge charge, ensure a gentler ride. Even so, he could still achieve an acceleration of fifteen times the force of gravity. Three live ejections were made in 1961 using this method, the first demonstrating its 'zero/zero' capability; that is to say, ejection at no forward speed and no height, as from a stationary plane on a runway. The parachutist who performed this was shot so far into the air that he could float down for 200ft (61m) with his canopy fully open. A new and demanding challenge came with the Vertical Take-Off and Landing (VTOL) aircraft, such as the P1127, the Hawker Siddeley Harrier, produced in 1966. What chance would a pilot have of reaching the ground alive from such a plane which might, if suffering engine trouble, drop vertically and thus negate the ejection seat's powerful thrust? Martin used the Dassault Test Rig at Vélizy, near Paris, to test the seats under high sink rate. Later, he designed a twenty-degree inclined track to demonstrate ejection from an aircraft diving at low altitude.

During the 1950s and 1960s, in recognition of his achievements, Martin received numerous awards including, from a grateful nation, the OBE, CBE and in 1965 a knighthood. He died in 1981, and is buried in Old Denham churchyard a short way from his company's headquarters, where he spent most of his working life. His company, a world leader in its field, continues his work unabated, pursuing a continuous search for improvement, as designs have had to be constantly modified in line with changes in aircraft systems and their more demanding capability and function. And Sir James Martin's name lives on at Denham too: the company's joint managing directors are his two sons, John and James.

Over the years, the ejection seat has come to incorporate many new accessories. A time-release unit ensures that the drogue parachute transfers its pull to the main 24ft (7.3m) canopy at exactly the right moment. A barostat, automatically operated by air pressure, was also introduced. In a high-altitude ejection this prevents the main parachute from opening until a certain height is reached, normally 10,000ft (3,050m). Before that point, the escaping airman receives oxygen from the seat's built-in supply, switched on the moment he is ejected from the plane. This device, developed earlier by the Irvin company, was used to good effect over Derbyshire in April 1958 when two RAF officers, Flt Lt John de Salis and Flg Off Patrick Lowe, made the highest-ever ejection seat escape. They were flying a Canberra bomber, specially designed to collect radioactive samples over hydrogen bomb explosions, when at 57,000ft (17,385m) their plane suddenly blew apart, and they ejected. The temperature was a deadly minus 70°F, and the air dangerously lacking in oxygen. The barostat allowed the pair to fall in their seats for nine miles while they breathed the oxygen supply. Then, at a pre-set height of 13,000ft, the barostat was automatically activated. The parachutes opened and, breathing easily, the two men landed with only minor injuries, such as frostbite.

The ejection seat has also had mechanical leg restraints introduced to stop an airman's legs flailing dangerously when the seat is fired out. It was found, too, that the main parachute could be opened more quickly for low-level escape if extra drogue parachutes were installed to assist it. There are two drogues in tandem: one twenty-two inches in diameter (the 'controller' drogue), and the main one five feet in diameter. This system reduces the delay between ejection and the snapping open of the main parachute. Another development has ensured that the parachute and rigging lines are automatically released if a landing is made in the sea. To make low-level escapes more risk-free, rocket motors, with one-inch diameter combustion tubes, are now routinely installed under seats to increase trajectory height. Two-inch diameter rockets are used in VTOL aircraft such as the Harrier to counteract their tendency to drop quickly if the engine fails, rather than glide to earth like other types of plane. These rockets can propel an airman as much as 450ft (137m) into the air – more than two and a half times the height of Nelson's Column. There is also an explosive cockpit canopy jettisoning system and, in the case of helicopters, a device that chops off the rotors so that they cannot obstruct the pilot and seat when they are shot out upwards. On later marks of seat, the face curtain has been replaced by a handle between the pilot's knees, which is much quicker to use.

The parachute used in Martin-Baker Mark 10 ejection seats is the GQ Aeroconical, produced by the company founded by James Gregory and Raymond Quilter in the 1930s. This incorporates a major refinement in its design: a shallow non-porous cone woven into the canopy, which speeds opening while reducing shock. Mark 12 seats, such as those installed in the Harrier and the Taiwanese Ching Kuo fighter, use Irvin's Automatic Inflation Modulation (AIM) parachute. This aids development by employing a small inner parachute that is acted upon by the air flow into the canopy and produces tension on the rigging lines. A number of ejection seats also employ Irvin drogues. Martin-Baker's Mark 10 ejection seat is virtually the standard Western zero/zero model, having been installed in forty-three different aircraft types in a total of sixty-one air forces throughout the world – an impressive achievement.

The complex technology of the latest super-armchairs enables them to perform a dozen mechanical and electronic tasks almost simultaneously and with remarkable precision, setting in train a tightly programmed sequence. Improvements have now shrunk the time lapse between the pilot's emergency tug on the striped handle between his knees and parachute deployment to less than half a second. But no matter how sophisticated the technology no rescue device can cope with the unforeseen, the inevitable occasional strokes of bad luck due to weather or human error. Hence the constant striving after refinements and improvements. The latest models, the Navy Aircrew Common Ejection Seat (NACES), are now employing computers with a unique digital electronically controlled sequencer. Hundreds have been supplied by Martin-Baker to the US Navy. Ejection seats are made too by the US, Russia and China, though Martin-Baker has secured three quarters of the Western market. One of their latest seats, M16A, is fitted to the new Eurofighter 2000.

Although the saving of life is the ejection seat's principal purpose, governments are not so soft-hearted as to ignore their account books and the cost of accidents to the taxpayer, for saving lives also saves money. Hence the cold equation that investing in a single ejection seat costing between £80,000 and £120,000 can save a pilot who has cost perhaps £7 million to train, plus another £3 million in the case of an experienced pilot. The plane – and one in every ten military aircraft crashes, largely through engine failure – is a write-off anyway. Most of us, not being accountants, can appreciate in simple human terms the impressively high percentage of rescues: today, ninety-six out of every hundred pilots who eject with Sir James Martin's brilliant 'bang seat' parachute to safety. The remaining four may have ejected too low or too late, or not survived for many other reasons not directly attributable to the seat. Since 1949, more than 6,500 aircrew have pulled down the seat's face-blind or tugged its lower firing handle, consigned themselves to the winds and survived to tell the tale.

CHAPTER FOURTEEN

THE FUN JUMPERS

M odern sports parachuting, particularly skydiving, has evolved indirectly from the show jumpers of the 1930s. It was the day of experiment with the delayed drop and the so-called 'bird-men' who, with canvas 'wings' webbing their outstretched arms and legs, leapt from aircraft to cavort about the sky until, thousands of feet later, they descended on their parachutes to the crowds' applause for their panache and daring.

But not always. For the bird-men's careers tended to be short, often ending in death. When the American Clem Sohn took part in a display at Hanworth airfield near Twickenham in May 1936, he survived a drop from 10,000ft (3,050m), gliding until he was 1,000ft (305m) from the ground. Less than a year later, however, at Vincennes in France, he died when his main parachute caught up on one of his 'wings' and, like his reserve, failed to open. More recently, in May 1956, tragedy befell Leo Valentin, a thirty-seven-year-old French bird-man who in his time made more than 600 parachute jumps and used 'wings' of balsa wood and alloy fitted with ailerons. At the International Air Pageant at Liverpool airport, Valentin made one thrilling delayed drop from a Dakota, then flew again and made another jump. But this time he hit the side of the plane as he left it. Officials realised something was wrong when his parachute began to open after only 1,000ft (305m) of freefall. It failed to deploy properly and, watched by 100,000 people, the bird-man dropped helplessly through space and was killed outright two miles from the airfield.

A serious attempt at high-altitude freefall was part of a US Air Force research project in 1960 which resulted in a remarkable world record for the courageous officer Capt Joseph W. Kittinger. On 16 August he left Holloman Base in New Mexico in the gondola of a helium balloon and jumped at 102,000ft (31,110m), a height which gave him an uninterrupted view of the earth's surface for 400 miles (644km). Although at times he experienced a choking sensation, Kittinger was in control of all his faculties during his descent. The freefall drop of 84,700ft (25,800m) was made with the aid of a stabilising drogue, and his barostatically controlled main parachute opened at 17,000ft (5,185m) after the four-and-a-half-minute plunge through space – a record that remains unbroken.

In the past two or three decades, parachute jumping for pleasure has graduated from guesswork to high accuracy, thanks to a technology which has transformed the parachute from a simple means of landing safely to a precision instrument, manufactured with an increasingly fine regard for aerodynamics. The parachute itself has adopted strange guises – puzzling to the layman, sought after by sportsmen eager for adventure beyond that offered by the familiar and traditional white mushroom. In recent years the skies have been peppered with a variety of canopies: triangular, heart-shaped, some with a tattered look but in fact the result of aerodynamic arrangement of slots and skirts, culminating in a new breed of versatile 'flying mattress' known as the ram-air. This is so speedy, steerable and versatile that even hardened parachutists see little scope for further radical advances in design, as distinct from minor modifications. Raised expectations from improved parachute technology have been matched by more demanding standards in competitive sport jumping. Some have become familiar to television and film audiences and spectators at skydiving exhibitions featuring, for example, the Red Devils or the Falcons, the display teams of the Parachute Regiment and the RAF respectively. Competitions in skydiving, also known as Formation Skydiving (FS), involve groups of four, eight or more jumpers forming as many different groups as possible against the clock. New variations on the sport parachute scene are sky-surfing and freestyle skydiving, 'stacking' (canopy formation) and para-skiing, which first featured in world competitions in 1996. As with ice-skating, presentation is all, and because performances are judged using photography – a skilled technique in itself – a videographer forms part of the team and shares in any awards.

Twenty years ago the best performances were largely achieved using manoeuvrable round parachutes such as the Para-Commander (a product of the US Pioneer Company and probably the most popular sport parachute in Britain and the US at the time, and still in use). Its British companions were Irvin's Delta II Parawing and Skydriver, GQ's Pathfinder and, a major challenger to the

Para-Commander, France's Papillon. The Para-Commander is essentially a traditionally shaped round parachute; its distinction lay in the lowered apex and a series of rear drive and turn slots which allowed air to escape, enabling control with some manoeuvrability and forward speed. The Papillon's competitive edge lay in its highly controllable sink rate, which made for particular accuracy when touching down. This parachute was in turn successfully challenged by the Competition Commander.

But time and technology have moved on. The ram-air, known colloquially but inaccurately as a 'square' but actually an arched rectangle, has revolutionised parachuting not only as a sport but as a factor in military preparedness. Its effectiveness is due to its resemblance in cross-section to an aircraft wing – an aerofoil – and is influenced by the four principal forces involved in flight: thrust and lift striving to counteract drag and weight. It is interesting historically, for this is the point where engineless aircraft, i.e. gliders and parachutes, meet, the common factor being the aerofoil, the key to flight itself. The ram-air parachute has upper and lower skins separated by cells. Air enters at the front, and the high pressure that builds up in the cells, which are sealed at the end, keeps them inflated. It is the parachute's forward movement that keeps the air 'rammed' into these cells. If the parachutist applies too much brake, the canopy would deflate and collapse, re-inflating when the brake is released; hence considerable skill is needed to use one. The ram-air reacts to air in a similar way to an aeroplane's wing. In forward movement, air moves rapidly over the tapering curve of the canopy's upper surface, producing low pressure, and comparatively slowly across the flatter lower surface, creating high pressure. The difference between these two pressures produces the lift, not enough to create the buoyancy of a balloon but enough partly to neutralise the drag and weight of the parachute and the jumper. Result: the parachute descends, but more slowly. In descent, a parachutist can enhance the ram-air's aerofoil effect by pulling on its lines at the rear, which will alter the air flow and its lift capabilities as well as induce turns. The parachute's high manoeuvrability and rapid response to braking means that jumpers can drop in brisker winds and to gentler landings.

Rules for sport parachuting's world championships are laid down by the Fédération Aéronautique Internationale and the International Parachuting Commission (IPC), and in the UK by the British Parachute Association, which is the sport's controlling body and is responsible for organising training and maintaining safety standards. Competition jumping demands keen judgement and knowledge, gained through training and experience, of a parachute's capabilities as a vehicle, which can glide, brake and be steered at will. The canopy nylon of the sport parachute is more tightly woven than that of the conventional emergency parachute, making the fabric less porous. Depending upon the type of parachute used, the air that would have permeated the canopy is forced out, in descent, through a series of slots, producing a mild form of jet propulsion. By manipulating the toggles attached to a parachute's rigging lines, the highly skilled jumper can home in on a small target disc with remarkable precision.

Progress in parachute design has been accompanied by greater personal attainments and stiffer criteria; for example, the introduction of smaller and smaller targets. In 1962, when the Sixth World Championships were held in Orange, Massachusetts, the dead-centre disc in the accuracy competitions was a cardboard plate 10in (25.4cm) in diameter. Competitors gained points for landing within 100ft (30.5m) of the target centre, most of the best performers landing within about 10ft (3m) of it. Within a few years, the centre spot had shrunk to 4in (10cm) in diameter, then to 1.97in (5cm). Now this has been almost halved to 1.18in (3cm). Scoring is on the basis of the number of perfect hits achieved out of ten, with distances being measured from the centre on a larger, electronically sensitive base. In general, parachuting is a participant rather than spectator sport since, apart from accuracy and canopy formation competitions, the action takes place out of sight of spectators – unless they use binoculars. That said, it is exciting to watch jumper and parachute in the accuracy rounds, steering and manoeuvring with deceptive ease time after time from perhaps 3,500ft (1,067m).

Style jumping, the other element of the classic events, is also a test of individual achievement in which accuracy of landing plays only a minor role. The skill lies in performing six pre-determined manoeuvres during freefall after leaving the aircraft and on reaching a terminal speed of descent of about 120mph (193kph), depending on mid-air posture. In the British championships, stylists leap from the plane at about 6,600ft (2,000m) and must not delay opening the parachute for more than twenty-five seconds. They stabilise themselves in a 'frog' or semi-spread-eagle position, face down, then move into a programme of 360° turns and backward loops. Points are awarded for speed and precision and deducted for unfinished or incorrect manoeuvres. Style jumping by individuals gave birth to the kind of freefall activity known as formation skydiving, or relative work (RW), weaving human configurations thousands of feet up, taking perhaps less than a minute to form and disband before parachutes deploy and jumpers touch down. Sequential relative work, which is the performance of a set number of prescribed formations against the clock, is now a competition feature. Gliding towards each other, the skydivers join hands to form circles, stars and formations in ever-increasing numbers. The latest (unofficial) record for a freefall formation was created by 216 skydivers from twenty-three countries over Bratislava (Slovakia) at 21,000ft (6,405m) in 1994. Another impressive world record was set in the canopy formations discipline, stacking. Parachutists under their canopies stacked at an almost vertical angle, producing a figure resembling a flight of stairs. According to the *Guinness Book of Records*, the highest stack of parachutists so far is forty-six, achieved by an international team at Davis (California) in 1994. They held it for 37.54 seconds.

Skydivers are constantly on the lookout for variety and 'creativity' in their jumping. The latest variation is sky-surfing which, as yet in its infancy, originated in France and is thought to have developed from parachuting on to mountainsides while wearing skis. While traditional skydivers fall in a frog or spread-eagle position, face down, the sky-surfer descends from a plane at a considerable height, say 13,000ft (3,965m), 'standing' upright on his adaptation of a surfboard – a posture which in itself involves balancing skill. Then he performs a range of manoeuvres: tumbling, looping, flying diagonally, on the surfboard, and somersaulting. In 1995, three sky-surfers set up a world record by exiting their balloon at 20,000ft (6,100m), switching on their oxygen supply until they reached 10,000ft (3,050m). Another competition variation is freeflying, which consists of designing a series of do-your-own-thing performance routines, as long as it is interesting or entertaining. One form consists of a pair of competitors giving less than a minute's interactive display – a kind of aerial ballet *pas de deux* with points awarded for artistic merit and technical prowess.

Like most sports, parachuting involves much application and concentrated training to succeed, but most devotees of the sport are content to enjoy jumping at club level for the fun of it. To share the excitement of competition, or indeed orthodox sport parachuting at all, jumpers in the UK join the British Parachute Association which has nearly 3,700 individual members in thirty-four affiliated and associated parachuting clubs and centres. The subscription of

£55 a year includes an insurance package with third-party cover of up to £1 million. The first full-time commercial sport parachute training centre, still going strong, was opened at Sibson airfield near Peterborough (Cambs) in 1971 by John Meacock, a former world-class and many times national, style and accuracy champion. An ex-Territorial Army paratrooper, Meacock is a former chairman and vice-president of the BPA, and was awarded the Royal Aero Club's silver medal in recognition of his work for the sport. He himself is a veteran of more than 4,000 jumps, and although his career in competitive sport may be over, he has trained plenty of others – more than 36,000 jumpers in twenty-five years. As Meacock points out, there is a choice of route into sport parachuting. One for the uncertain is making a preliminary tandem jump, known in the United States, where it originated, as a 'buddy' jump. After only a few minutes' preparation, a complete tyro can be an instant parachutist – while attached by dual harness to an experienced instructor, who rides piggy-back and does all the work and carries the responsibility for the descent. After leaving the plane at about 10,000ft (3,050m), you both drop through about half a minute of freefall, then at about 5,000ft (1,525m) the instructor opens a large ram-air parachute and both land on it together. A reserve is naturally supplied. The one-off tandem jump would cost in the region of £160.

There are three recognised training methods, all employing main and reserve canopies, the latter equipped with an emergency automatic opening device. If your main parachute should fail, this gadget, activated by air pressure, detonates a cutter at about 1,000ft (305m) which severs the container retaining loop, allowing a small pilot 'chute to draw out the reserve. When the novice becomes proficient, the automatic opening device is an option worth serious consideration, despite its cost of several hundred pounds. Most experienced jumpers consider this a small but worthwhile addition to the average cost of kitting themselves out with main and reserve parachute, container and gear, which will last them years. There is also an additional outlay of around £5 and £13–£16 a time for jumps from 2,500ft and 12,000ft (762m and 3,660m) respectively.

Conventional Static Line

With this method your parachute would be the traditional round model, not a ram-air canopy. The main parachute is hauled from the backpack by static line when you jump. These jumps would go towards the BPA's initial (and essential) eight-level training progression. To reduce risks, you would not be allowed to jump in any wind brisker than 10 knots (11.5mph), and you should always be prepared to make old-fashioned roll-over landings. Thirty training descents could qualify you as 'experienced'. Cost: first jump around £120, then each subsequent one £18, including loan of equipment, although fees will vary from club to club.

Ram-Air Progression System (RAPS)

The most popular static-line method in use today. It utilises the state-of-the-art ram-air (square) parachute and comes complete with a harness and container system that positions both the main and reserve parachute in a single backpack container. BPA instructors would maintain a continuous jump assessment, moving you on to the next stage only when they feel it justified. Rapid proficiency could enable you to be freefalling on the seventh jump, adding manoeuvres in freefall until after about thirty jumps you could qualify as a skydiver. Then the sky's your oyster. You have immediate use of the ram-air instead of having to complete conversion training from the traditional round canopy, and you could jump in winds up to 15 knots (17mph). Cost: first jump up to £190, then £30 a time. Again, fees will vary from club to club.

Accelerated Freefall (AFF)

Some instructors believe this is the best and quickest way to the real thing for the serious skydiver-to-be. Your first skydive in, say, a week's course of eight to ten jumps would be from 12,000ft (3,660m), with up to forty-five seconds of freefall. You would be accompanied by two approved instructors (each of whom must have made at least 1,000 jumps and spent a total of ten hours in freefall), and a video photographer. Cost: £1,200–£1,300 for a course of eight jumps plus tandem skydive.

The Services make special provision for adventurous training parachute courses for volunteers from within their ranks, and at no cost to themselves, at the two Joint Service Parachute Centres at Netheravon (Wilts) and Weston-on-the-Green (Oxon), and

144

at similar centres in Germany and Cyprus. This is in line with the policy of providing Army, Navy and RAF personnel with adventure training as a means of encouraging fitness and initiative in peacetime. The centres take parachuting seriously and have produced teams proficient enough to have won the national team accuracy championship for six consecutive years. They also enter a team in the world championships. The aim of the Joint Service basic freefall parachute courses is fifteen jumps in three weeks. There are ten basic courses a year – forty-five people on each course drawn from all three Services. After the course, if they decide to continue parachute jumping they can do so, but at their own expense. The parachutes are US Mantas and GQ Pathfinders as mains – all ram-airs – with GQ's 5.5m Security Aeroconicals as reserves on the piggy-back harness and container system. Initial training includes preliminary jumps from a 12ft (3.7m) platform in an aircraft hangar, stepping off while holding on to handles. A fan causes drag and brings you to the ground in realistic conditions but under cover. This is followed by six static-line descents from an aircraft at 3,500ft (1,067m), of which the last three must show convincing pulls using a dummy ripcord. Only when this is achieved well can students graduate to freefall. 'The difference between our training and that provided by the Parachute Regiment is the arduous combat fitness training required for airborne soldiers,' says Major Bob Card, the Netheravon Centre's Commandant. 'Parachuting is basically a means of delivery. All Service people are capable of parachuting, so we provide just that. But many of them do go on to become paratroops, and those who pass our course have it recorded on their documents.' He adds: 'In a peacetime army the fighting challenge is missing, so adventurous training is considered an essential part of Service life. Parachuting figures among a number of challenge pursuits, including mountaineering, gliding and hang-gliding.'

The excitement of flinging oneself into space and landing safely has appealed to generations of parachutists since Garnerin jumped into the unknown 200 years ago. It is not without risk, but risk is kept to a minimum through sport parachuting's controlling body, the British Parachute Association. It constantly lays emphasis on high-quality equipment and sound training in its attempts to cut avoidable accidents. The fact is that equipment is less fallible than the human being using it. Fatalities are rare, and injuries commonly no more serious than a twisted ankle or broken limb. 'We have to accept that as in football and other sports we will never stop injuries completely, but of course we have to be realistic,' says John Hitchen, National Coach and Safety Officer of the British Parachute Association. 'The modern parachute has reduced injuries, but what normally causes an accident is the jumper, not the equipment.' Rodger Tamblyn, a typical experienced club member with more than 500 parachute jumps to his credit, agrees, but adds: 'Most parachutists believe that a little bit of fear makes the adrenalin flow, and it's the adrenalin in your system that speeds your reactions. It makes the brain work faster – you can work out problems very quickly and it heightens awareness. Instructors always say that if you don't have a slight element of fear you might make a mistake through being blasé.' Tamblyn himself has been involved in two parachuting accidents, and readily admits blame in both. In one case his canopy collapsed at treetop height. 'I steered over the top of a tree to avoid parked cars, but left it too late and got slightly hurt.' Rodger Tamblyn is a parachuting photographer, which adds to the risk: it's another responsibility to be borne in mind, something else to think about. His second accident was a whiplash injury caused by the weight of his camera positioned on his head. 'I probably wasn't experienced enough to slow the opening of the parachute – there are ways of doing this, and I wasn't familiar enough with them.'

It was a mistake resulting from inexperience that involved that dashing entrepreneur Richard Branson in mid-air difficulties at Netheravon in 1987, when he was taking an accelerated freefall course in preparation for a world balloon flight. Looking at this incident on television, one feared the worst. In fact, Branson was accompanied by two highly skilled instructors who were his airborne guardians; the photographer's presence was a routine obligation during training. During Branson's jump, instead of pulling the ripcord he pulled a handle which would have jettisoned his main parachute. One of his instructors spotted what had happened, and promptly moved in and operated his reserve's ripcord handle for him. If Branson was temporarily unnerved, so were Virgin's shareholders. Like Branson, the shares dived, wiping 15p off their price and £15 million off the value of his company.

Bad luck in parachuting has frequently had deadly results, but as one skydiver told the author, 'If the number of people injured or killed on horseback had died parachuting, our sport would have been banned years ago.' But bad luck has often been neutralised by the good luck of last-second rescues, such as the spectacular one made in 1994 by skydiver Andy Peckett, a company director from Purton (Wilts) and a former member of the Royal Marines freefall team. Peckett was taking part in a formation drop by a team of twenty-four in a festival at Vichy, near Paris, when he saved the life of his friend Maurizio Brambilla, an Italian skydiver. Brambilla was among the first to leave the Hercules transport plane, but was knocked unconscious on the side of it as he exited at 15,000ft (4,575m). He was hurtling towards the ground when Peckett spotted him in difficulties. Leaping out, Peckett put his head down to minimise air resistance and dived 11,000ft (3,355m) towards his friend. When he caught him, he hooked his arm in Brambilla's straps and opened his parachute for him – at about ten seconds from the ground. Peckett then opened his own parachute at 2,000ft (610m), and both landed safely. Peckett's quick thinking and courage later earned him the Royal Humane Society's bronze medal.

It was bad luck too that nearly deprived the parachuting world of one of its most accomplished performers, Jackie Smith – now Mrs Young – who was the first woman member of the famous Red Devils, the Parachute Regiment's freefall team. She was taking part in a show in a small arena in Swansea in 1972. 'When diving out of the aircraft,' she told me, 'I caught the top of my parachute pack – a B4 military surplus backpack – and bent the top pin, making the ripcord impossible to pull. I had no option but to pull my reserve handle, but the reserve not only inverted but "blew" thirteen panels, making my descent very fast and uncontrollable. Luckily, I landed in Mumbles Harbour, about 400 yards [366m] out to sea, and I was saved from drowning by my lifejacket. A team-mate, Steve Slater, swam out to my rescue and a little boat came chugging past and a lady asked if we wanted a lift – as though we were at a bus-stop!'

Today, Jackie looks back on a brilliant career in sport parachuting, which was stimulated while serving with the Women's Royal Army Corps. 'At Aldershot I used to watch the paras jumping from the barrage balloon on Queen's Avenue, and had an urge to do it myself.' So she signed on for a four-jump basic parachute course at the Joint Service Parachute Centre at Netheravon, went on a fifteen-jump continuation course, entered the Army Parachute Championships and won the Novices event. She then accepted an invitation to join the Red Devils, creating a precedent by being its first female member. 'There was a fat file containing some of the most incredible reasons why I shouldn't be allowed in,' she says. 'One was that if I jumped on displays and flew over the crowd everyone would be able to see up my skirt!' But Jackie was eventually taken on strength, and in March 1972 became a fully-fledged Red Devil, despite grumblings by some who felt the presence of a woman would detract from the ruggedness of the Parachute Regiment's macho image. 'But after I started competing with the "blokes" and beating most of them, I think I can honestly say they all looked upon me as a little sister – and I had the best family in the world.' Jackie Smith spent five years globe-trotting, giving performances with the Red Devils and training with the US Army parachute team, the Golden Knights, at Fort Bragg (North Carolina). Back in the UK, the Red Devils attended every meeting they could, claiming abundant gold medals in team and individual events, and in 1978 Jackie won what she calls 'the most prestigious medal of all', which took her into the *Guinness Book of Records*.

She was a member of the British team competing in the World Parachuting Championships at Zagreb. Having proved in accuracy training that she could hit dead centres (at that time a 10cm target disc), she was on tenterhooks under competition conditions, which were 'so different'. Weather and air turbulence were causing delays, adding to the stress. As the contest continued, Jackie excitedly realised she had scored nine perfect hits on the electronic pad. *Calm, calm, calm . . . Slow down the breathing . . . Get a grip.* 'All these things were going through my mind. I just felt terribly sick, but had to get on with the task of trying to get just one more dead-centre. My parachute took what seemed like ages to open. Not knowing what the conditions were like, I set up my final approach far too close to the pit and had to do some really radical corrections to take my parachute to where I wanted it . . . Descending through the last 20ft [6m], I could feel – and worst of all, see – my left foot twitching as the ground came up to meet me. I saw the bright orange disc – dead centre – and opted to use my still-in-control right foot. The next point of contact was my backside . . . It seemed like an eternity waiting for the electronic read-out. When the figures 0.00 lit up, I just lay back in the pea gravel, not believing I had done it.' But done it she had, becoming the first and only person in the world, male or female, to score ten consecutive dead-centres in the world championships. Since then, Jackie has represented Britain seven times in the world event, winning more medals. She was also the first woman to wear the coveted Red Beret when she was attached to the Red Devils, and was awarded her golden lanyard on completing her first 1,000 jumps. To date she has logged around 4,000. But these days Jackie Young is grounded. Her husband, Dougie Young, is Sergeant-Major at the Joint Service Parachute Centre at Netheravon, where he teaches adventurous training to the Armed Services volunteers, and Jackie has full-time work of her own – and two young sons. She last jumped in 1995. 'But if ever again I feel the urge to get my knees in the breeze, then skydiving is still very accessible to me. Who knows, I may even make a comeback – if I'm not using a zimmer frame!'

With the coming of the ram-air ('square') parachute, with its aerofoil characteristics, the borderlines between one discipline and another in the parachute-jumping world have become increasingly blurred. The basic criterion for acceptability among the orthodox parachutists is that jumping is from the air, i.e. from an aircraft or balloon, which makes the new sport of sky-surfing – a form of 'stand-up' descent on a surfboard from as much as 10,000ft (3,500m) – acceptable, but not paragliding or hang-gliding, which are more akin to gliding than to parachute jumping. The pilots of new high-performance paragliders suspend themselves under what resemble aircraft wings or high-tech ram-airs, and take off from cliffs or hillsides. These special ram-airs have a high lift characteristic and a glide ratio of about twice the conventional parachute. Skilled users can exploit thermals – the patches of air which, warmed by the earth's surface, add to lift – making it possible to glide long distances. Travelling as much as 100 miles (161km) from base is not unusual.

Parascending is a branch of parachuting where, in ascent, the ram-air parachute acts rather like a glider, and in descent like a parachute. Over water, using the round parachute, parascending is the only form of parachuting which the public can enjoy without considerable training, though you can make a tandem jump, with an instructor, over land. Originally, in the early 1970s, the parascenders belonged to the British Parachute Association, but in 1973 they parted company and formed their own organisation, later becoming the British Hang-gliding and Paragliding Association, to which 600 parascending club members are affiliated and which is the sport's governing body. There are two kinds of parascending: on land, where you usually use a ram-air parachute and are hoisted into the air towed by a motor vehicle; and over water – either the sea or inland lakes – when you use a round parachute. Making a land-based take-off, you make a standing start at ground level, with the parachute held open by club members and so placed that its 'mouth' faces the towing vehicle, to which the parachute is attached by a line typically about 1,150ft (350m) long. It lies back along the ground and back to the parachute, which in turn is attached to the jumper's harness. The line's slack is taken up by the tow vehicle, usually a 4 × 4 motor vehicle which has all round visibility, and the parascender gently lifts to between 800ft and 1,000ft (264m and 305m). At the chosen height, you use a legs-apart signal to the driver that you want to release yourself. He stops the vehicle, allowing you to pull the cord activating the release mechanism. 'Because we use the ram-air parachute for parascending on land, and in view of its versatility, it obviously requires training,' says Arthur Bentley, chairman of Birdwings Parascending Club based at South Cerney (Glos). 'But anyone, as an introduction, can make a tandem jump with an instructor who will be in charge of the jump, ride piggy-back and operate the release mechanism. All that is required for this is a simple briefing.' What about the dangers? 'There obviously is a risk, but we've been operating since 1982 and have only had one broken ankle in that time,' he says. Cost: a trial tandem jump would cost about £10 a flight; membership of Arthur Bentley's Birdwings club, for example, is £68 per year – and to keep costs down they have equipped themselves with their own Land Rover for towing.

Over-land parascending has its serious side, to the extent of holding annual accuracy competitions, much along the lines of orthodox parachute jumping. Parascending, in its over-water form, uses slotted Para-Commander-type round parachutes, and is the only branch of parachuting in which the public can make pleasure jumps without taking a course of training. Training is required for land jumping, but over water novice parascenders galore can be seen soaring above the waves at the seaside after only a briefing – with a wetting in store at the end of it. Over-water parascending has been in operation since 1972. It can be seen in action at resorts round Britain's coastline, such as Sheerness, Exeter, Bournemouth, Torquay harbour, Millendreath (Cornwall) and other places in Scotland and Ireland. You ascend from pontoons – floating platforms moored just out from the shore – or are towed by towboat or winch boat, and up you go. Parascending costs about £18 for a flight of six to ten minutes. Helmets and lifebelts are the only essentials, and these are supplied. Parascending operators must qualify by passing an examination after a five- or seven-day course at a training centre approved by the British Hang-gliding and Paragliding Association. They may also hold a certificate in boat-handling competency as well as a first-aid certificate. For parascending over either land or sea, younger solo jumpers must be aged fourteen or over, have parents' approval, declare that they are in reasonable good health and that they are aware of the risk. 'As a precaution,' says Barry Clark of the Fly High Parascending Centre at West Malling (Kent), 'parascenders should always check that the operator and instructors are approved by the BHPA. That's your guarantee that they are properly trained and qualified.'

The most flamboyant and controversial successor to the exhibitionism of the early parachute experimenters is BASE jumping, BASE being an acronym for Buildings, Antennae (radio masts), Spans (bridges) and Earthbound objects. In Britain, these have included pylons, tall buildings such as hotels, Beachy Head, and even the Whispering Gallery of St Paul's Cathedral. The base jumpers have tended to disdain the warnings exemplified by the fate of twenty-five-year-old Darren Newton, who in 1992 died when jumping from the twenty-eighth floor of the London Hilton Hotel in Park Lane. His parachute failed to open. An inquest heard that the jumper had his head down instead of up, and appeared to catch his foot in the guide ropes. He struck the building with 'tremendous force', plummeted 300ft (91m) and hit a wall before smashing into a canopy, severing an arm.

The high risk of such jumps, performed at low level, coupled with the risk of capricious wind patterns around buildings that shrinks the margin of error, inflates the base jumper's psyche and the excitement. The coroner, Dr Paul Knapman, recording a verdict of accidental death, said that base jumpers were 'trespassers who put the lives of others at risk'. But for base jumpers, danger appears to be addictive. More than three years later Gary Bullock did the same jump, surviving to write in the magazine *Sports in the Sky* of his 'overwhelming elation and a very distinct taste of the ever present drug, adrenalin' as he landed in Park Lane's central reservation. Not surprisingly, orthodox jumpers are strongly opposed to base jumping, not only because it leads to unnecessary deaths and injuries, but because its controversial reputation tends to tarnish the safety-first image of the mainstream sport. And safety first is anything but an attraction for the base jumpers.

The British Parachute Association's operations manual says that activities such as fixed object jumping are outside their interest; they are concerned with parachute jumping from objects that move, e.g aircraft and balloons. Nor are they interested in trespassing on other people's property to do it. The world record height for a base jump is 19,300ft (5,880m) from a ledge in the Karakoram Range in Pakistan in 1992, but the *Guinness Book of Records*, anxious not to appear to encourage base jumping, prudently warns that 'jumps from buildings and claims for lowest base jumps will not be accepted'.

Another trend which appears to be attracting unfortunate publicity to sports jumpers is making sponsored parachute jumps for charity by novices, often not properly trained. One Hampshire club, which sent four sponsored charity jumpers into hospital, angered a local surgeon who complained at the pressure that hospital resources were being put under by parachutists. 'People who are attracted to these weekend jumps by a desire to sponsor various forms of charity may perhaps raise £200 a time, but it could cost the National Health Service £2,000 to £3,000 for £100-a-day stays in hospital.'

Useful Addresses

British Parachute Association, 5 Wharf Way, Glen Parva, Leicester LE2 9TF. (Tel: 01162 785271).
British Hang-gliding & Paragliding Association, The Old Schoolroom, Loughborough Rd, Leicester LE4 5PJ (Tel: 01162 611322).
Birdwings Parascending Club, c/o 37 Dovetrees, Carterton, Oxon OX18 1AW.
Fly High Sky Sports, 101 Heath Road, Barming, Maidstone, Kent ME16 9DR.
Joint Service Parachute Centre, Airfield Camp, Netheravon, Wilts SP4 9SF. (Tel: 01980 678245).
Peterborough Parachute Centre, Sibson Airfield, Wansford, Peterborough PE8 6NE. (Tel: 01832 280490).

CHAPTER FIFTEEN

OUT OF THIS WORLD

When he was Prince of Wales, the late Duke of Windsor, often flew with the RAF. One day, while he was putting on his parachute before a flight, somebody asked him if he knew how to use it. 'No,' he said, 'and I don't want to.' Perhaps the Prince thought that a little knowledge might tempt Providence into giving him cause to use it. But he need not have worried; he never had to. Thirty years later, however, his successor, Prince Charles, had no qualms at all about parachutes. In 1977 he became Colonel-in-Chief of the Parachute Regiment, and the following year qualified as a military parachutist at No. 1 Parachute Training School, Brize Norton (Oxon), one of 170,000 troops who have trained there since 1940.

In the 1970s, however, although paratroop training methods and equipment had not changed in essence in thirty years, they did so in important details. Irvin's PX parachute was bigger than the old X type – 32ft (9.8m) in flat diameter instead of 28ft (8.5m), thus giving a slower, steadier drop. And it acquired a fourteen-inch net skirt to prevent blown peripheries, a type of malfunction causing part of the canopy to twist inside out and produce dangerously rapid descents. In 1955, paratroops began carrying a reserve in addition to their main parachute, but this may one day disappear again as, except in training, the PX1 Mark 4 round parachute gradually gives way to the highly manoeuvrable ram-air.

No. 1 Parachute Training School, formerly at Ringway, puts professional paratroops and foreign trainees through their paces with a four-week basic course – two weeks for the Territorials – at Brize Norton. In a huge hangar, recruits are literally given a firm grounding in aircraft drill, flight and landing techniques with the aid of harnesses suspended from the roof, jumping platforms, a Hercules fuselage on the ground to give exiting experience, and a fan trainer suspended 40ft above the hangar floor to produce a realistic rate of descent. Then come one static line drop at 1,000ft

153

(305m) from an aircraft – a Short Skyvan – in flight, three more daytime descents, one night jump and three drops with equipment, the last at 800ft (244m). The load is suspended below the trainee, so that in hitting the ground first it momentarily checks the rate of his fall. Gone, though, are the once-standard, once-feared drops from a cage beneath a balloon at 800ft (244m), though this relic lingered on until 1995. 'The old balloon was less cost-effective and just tested your confidence,' says Sqn Ldr Roland Wadley, officer i/c the Training Co-ordination and Resources Flight at Brize Norton. And long since gone are the hated Whitleys and Wellingtons, bombers converted for often bloody drops through funnels in the fuselage floor, now merely curiosities to be read about in the School's histories by new-generation paras.

Training discipline is firmly and wisely maintained. It has to be; airborne operations must be left to chance as little as possible. Through the training hangar hubbub of shouted orders shines the message crystallised in the school's motto, 'Knowledge Dispels Fear', and that of the Parachute Regiment, 'Utrinque Paratus', 'Ready for Anything'. The Parachute Jumping Instructors (PJIs) are furnished as always by the RAF, drawn from the Physical Education branch. 'You develop great trust in your PJI,' says a typical young trainee para. 'They're all very good teachers – they're confident, patient, correct at all times and slowly they instil you with confidence.' The initial ordeal of leaping into space is a personal challenge that sometimes proves too much. Refusal by a trainee to jump is not the military offence it would be for a fully-fledged paratrooper, but with a regard for his own safety and that of his potential comrades-in-arms in operational conditions he is not given a second chance, but is quietly returned to his original unit. Training after the basic course is specialised, depending on whether a para is destined for the Special Air Service (SAS), Royal Marines or becoming a PJI. He might well need a further six-week course, which would include freefall training for operations.

A new generation of versatile post-war parachutes now meets more ambitious operational demands, and the highly manoeuvrable ram-air parachute, familiar to sport parachutists, can be used. For covert operations, such as dropping troops behind enemy lines, and as a result of experiments begun in the 1960s using freefall, special High Altitude Low Opening (HALO) parachutes have appeared. GQ's 360 tactical system, designed for drop heights up to 25,000ft (7,625m), is intended for day or night special forces operations by troops carrying full combat equipment. Each paratrooper carries his own oxygen supply during the long drop until his 'hitefinder' barometric device automatically deploys his parachute. Loads of supplies, each of 353lb (160kg), descend separately, but paras can steer themselves to the equipment during freefall so that all land together. This canopy can also be used in the High Altitude High Opening (HAHO) mode, using a static line. The parachute opens as the jumper leaves the aircraft, and he can steer and glide long distances to his dropping zone – twenty miles has been recorded – allowing the plane to make for base without having to fly over the target. The low-level version can be used from drops of only 1,000ft (305m), a great advantage when Marines, for example, drop and rendezvous with a rigid inflatable boat on a dropping zone within range of their target. To make aircraft less vulnerable to attack at the usual paratroop dropping height of 800ft (244m), aircraft can now fly in at 250ft (76m) using special low-level static-line parachutes which are rapid openers. GQ's is conical; Irvin's, like the Russell Lobe, is shallow and curls under at the edges.

Whatever a parachute's purpose and whoever is destined to use it, intensive efforts are routinely made to ensure its fitness for its job. No visitor to a parachute factory, with its long tables where parachutes in the making are laid out, can fail to be struck by two factors: first, its silence, punctuated only by the low whirring of sewing machines as seamstresses stitch together the canopy gores and panels; and, second, the paramount preoccupation with the safe assembly of the product. For the government sets high standards. Each parachute company must work to a quality assurance system, headed by a manager approved by the Defence Quality Assurance Board. On his staff is a team comprising around twenty per cent of the factory's strength, which conducts stringent tests and spot checks right down the production line. Is the canopy fabric of the right porosity and tensile strength? Are the emergency parachute's gores and panels firmly sewn? Are the rigging lines the prescribed length measured at the correct tension? Is the parachute well packed; has a thorough job been made of the repair to that torn parachute? Check . . . counter-check . . . tested and approved, with the conviction that if any injury or accident does occur, it will not be due to bad workmanship or incorrect manufacture. Parachutes are no longer produced only in white. NATO air forces colour them in four vertical segments from apex to hem: khaki, sand, white and international orange. On landing, the pilot can either camouflage his presence or make himself conspicuous, depending on circumstances and terrain, by laying the parachute on the ground with the appropriate colour uppermost. At Irvin's factory they have an additional task. At one time airborne forces parachutes were serviced and re-packed by the RAF; but today this has been contracted to be carried out at Letchworth (Herts).

Emergency parachutes, described in previous chapters, have changed much over the years as designs have been adapted to the ejection seat, invented to facilitate escapes from high-speed aircraft. Since the parachute was officially adopted by the government for the RAF in the 1920s, civil aviation has never found a place for it; the Civil Aviation Authority makes no regulations governing its use. If this is surprising, bear in mind that most air accidents occur on take-off or landing, when a parachute would be useless. And even if an accident occurred at a height where the air outside was breathable, the idea of hundreds of jumbo jet passengers scrambling for the exits wearing parachutes they were not trained to use is absurd, even if the plane could tolerate the extra weight of hundreds of parachutes. But pilots of light aircraft and gliders are another matter. There are no CAA regulations covering parachute use in these either, but clubs themselves are more safety conscious than they were and see that pilots carry them if there is a likelihood of flying in cloud, across country, or performing aerobatics. Even as I write, a collision between two gliders has been reported in Gloucestershire, and the pilot of one saved his life using a parachute because he had been trained to do so. Most gliding accidents are mid-air crashes at sporting events, and parachutes are clearly of value here. Seating in gliders can be specially shaped to accommodate a parachute backpack, so an additional incentive to wearing one is the obvious discomfort of not doing so.

Twenty years ago, in the United States, came the idea of an aircraft safety detonating cord which would be used in conjunction with parachutes for accidents, such as engine failure, in flight. The idea was for the cord to 'parcel' the plane at intervals all round the fuselage. In an emergency, the pilot or crew member would pull a handle to explode the detonating cord, slicing the fuselage into neat segments, each of which would carry passengers down on its parachute. From time to time, attempts have been made to go the whole way and lower an entire aircraft by parachute to avoid a crash. As far back as 1910, J. F. Webb took out a British patent for a huge triple assembly of parachutes to be deployed one after the other by an 'air anchor', a kind of large dome-like auxiliary parachute, with the aircraft suspended beneath. Whether Webb's device was practicable or not is unknown, but eighteen years later a single parachute 84ft (25.6m) in diameter and strong enough to support a loaded plane was developed by the US Air Corps, similar to those used in moon module splashdowns during the Apollo programme. Parachutes for dropping light aircraft in their entirety are now a reality. In 1995 Cirrus, a company based in Duluth (Minnesota), designed the SR20 aircraft with an 80lb (36kg) parachute built into the top of the fuselage as standard equipment. If a plane suffered engine or structural failure, the pilot or crew would pull a handle in the cabin and a silk parachute would burst out from the plane's roof, deploy into a 30ft (9m) 'square', and slow the stricken four-seater to a 30mph (48kph) descent instead of a disastrous crash. Pressure-packed parachutes made of ribbon strips are now used to recover pilotless robot target or reconnaissance 'drones' after they have run out of fuel or finished their task. Guided missiles at the research and development stage also come down by parachute, though this is merely a revival of the system first used by the Germans during tests on their secret weapon, the V2 rocket bomb, in 1943.

For high-speed aircraft, parachutes perform a useful role as a braking device, one of three methods used to shorten the long landing run needed by high-speed planes, at the same time preventing wear on brakes and tyres. Some aircraft, for example on naval carriers, use arrester hooks on landing. Some have reverse-thrust engines, but these add greatly to weight, and a brake parachute makes a light and effective alternative. A canopy 31ft (9.5m) flat diameter was used on the prototype Concorde during the development stage, and parachutes have also been used to brake the Caravelle, a commercial aircraft, V-bombers Victor and Vulcan, and strike and fighter planes such as the Hunter, Jaguar, Lightning, Phantom and Hawk, and the new Eurofighter 2000. Many brake parachutes are composed of lengths of nylon ribbon stitched into concentric circles, with a gap between each. It is strong enough to withstand the enormous opening shock without damage, and will maintain its stability even if wet, when the fabric's porosity is reduced almost to nil. A small spring-loaded auxiliary parachute helps rapid deployment. Versions of the brake parachute are used by racing cars, particularly dragsters, which need to slow from 140 to 60mph (225 to 97kph). That Arnold Sundqvist, a twenty-six-year-old Swedish jet car driver, survived a crash in the 1970s was thanks to his parachutes. During a run-up to a flying quarter-mile during the World Speed Record Weekend at Elvington (Yorks) in October 1972, he was travelling at 300mph (483kph) when he swerved, ran off the runway for half a mile and crashed, slowing down as he did so. 'It was my two parachutes that saved me,' he said afterwards.

The parachute's retarding quality brings aircraft out of spins during testing, saving the lives of pilots and thousands, perhaps millions, of pounds in the cost of the plane. Normally an anti-spin parachute is assisted out of the rear of the fuselage by means of a gun. A steel slug is shot out at an angle, away from the air turbulence, taking with it an auxiliary parachute which pulls out the main canopy on a long strop. When the plane emerges from its stall, it goes into a steep dive and is thus under control, and the parachute can immediately be cut loose. Increased aircraft speeds have made the matter of dropping bombs at low levels risky because of the possibility of bomb fragments hitting the plane. To enable a plane to fly safely past a target zone, the bomb is slowed by parachute, which stabilises it for accurate trajectories and gives the aircraft a chance to move out of danger. The air inflatable retarder (AIR) parachute has four air inlets to provide high drag. Of several systems used in the Gulf War, one was designed primarily for use by the Tornado and was intended to prevent enemy use of an airfield. It comprises twin warheads which are dropped by parachute and dig into an airfield's surface. The first explodes, so does the second, deepening the crater made by the first. Another bomblet sits on the surface of the runway and explodes if vehicles or people approach. An anti-armour cluster bomb was parachuted down in the Falklands and Gulf Wars. This was so that any warhead targeting tanks or armoured vehicles would be designed to drop vertically, penetrating armour more effectively.

As an alternative to using conventional expensive pilotless aircraft as missile targets, the Irvin company developed a system using a supply container (as ballast) attached to a slow-falling parachute as used for dropping flares. The unique feature of this type was its silverised canopy, which could be tracked by radar. A similar version helped the Meteorological Office to keep a close watch on weather conditions in the stratosphere. Between 1963 and 1980, Skua rocket-sonde parachutes were fired from a station in South Uist in the Outer Hebrides, which received data on temperature and winds. A solid-propellant rocket, about eight feet (2.4m) long, was fired to an average height of forty-five miles

(72.44km). At its highest point, a small explosive charge forced off the nose cone, liberating a 15ft (4.6m) diameter parachute, which carried a sensor and a low-powered transmitter. The canopy was of fine silk so that it could be packed into as small a container as possible. It had thirty-two shaped gores coated alternately with a silverised copper finish, enabling radar tracking up to seventy-five miles (120km). As it descended, the wind direction could be calculated from its drift. The sensor registered changes in temperature, and these affected the pitch of its radio signal, which was picked up by receivers on the ground. The parachute rockets were fired regularly from a network of stations mainly in the earth's northern hemisphere. From the data they collected, meteorologists charted patterns of weather behaviour at various heights above the earth and discovered the causes of stratospheric disturbances, some of which were very severe, particularly in winter. Today the work of rocket-sonde parachutes has been taken over by radio-sondes. Stratospheric data is provided by Stornoway upper air station, where large balloons can ascend to high altitudes. The Met Office uses two types of drop-sonde, with parachutes only 19.7in (50cm) in diameter. One type is operated by the wind, the other by a thermal fuse.

Since the 1930s, new jobs have been found for man-carrying parachutes. The Russians, quicker than most to realise possibilities, established a twenty-man medical team to drop into remote areas of the country with personnel and supplies, and their example has since been followed in hitherto inaccessible spots the world over. Dropping medical supplies is also a function of the large and highly trained team of 400 'smoke jumpers', who since 1940 in the area of the Rockies and westwards as well as in other areas in the United States have rescued crew and passengers of crashed planes and fought forest fires. The smoke jumpers, based in Moussoula (Montana), tackle frequent outbreaks of fires, caused mostly by storm lightning, before they gain too devastating a hold. The fire fighters do not necessarily put fires out. Dropping from between 1,500ft (407m) and 2,000ft (710m), they try to contain the flames by creating breaks across which the fire cannot leap. This could mean burning undergrowth or digging trenches around the blaze's edges. 'We realise that sometimes letting fires burn on is a good thing,' says Wayne Williams of the US Forest Service. 'Years ago we thought all fires were bad, but renewal can actually improve wildlife habitats. Undergrowth is not a good habitat for wildlife, and fire is a natural predator of the insects that kill many useful timbers.' Smoke jumpers parachute from a 12ft (3.7m) static line attached to their aircraft. 'When they land they assess the situation and report whether fire-fighting gear needs to be flown in,' says Williams. 'But their principal role is to starve the fire of fuel by removing the undergrowth in its path.' In the case of a large fire, the aircraft, a turbine-engined DC-3, will use its infra-red cameras to reveal where the hottest spots are, because they are not always visible. The smoke jumpers have made 250,000 individual jumps of all kinds. The parachute they use is an FS14 with a parabolic canopy, which they find is more reliable than the square parachute. It is made in diameters of 28ft, 30ft and 32ft (8.5m, 9m and 9.6m) depending on the jumper's weight, has a top speed of 15mph (24kph) and is highly manoeuvrable. The reserve is a steerable FS12R with a 26ft (8m) diameter. The team has had its share of tragedies. 'In 1994 we lost three smoke jumpers in Colorado,' says Wayne Williams. 'In one case the jumper became entangled in his static line and broke his neck. Another landed in a tree two feet off the ground, broke away and accidentally hanged himself. While experimenting with a new system, a third jumper leapt out of the plane, but failed to pull his ripcord.' The worst disaster, however, occurred in 1949 when a blaze began in Mann Gulch in Montana. A crew of fifteen dropped above it, but tragically the fire went out of control and within two hours had taken its toll, killing twelve of the smoke jumpers and a district fireguard.

Over ten years in the 1960s, parachutes helped international communications when the Post Office, Cable & Wireless, and Standard Telephones & Cables used them to lay telephone cables on the sea bed. The parachute, made by RFD-GQ (predecessor of GQ Parachutes), helped to lower through the water a ten-foot-long torpedo-shaped device called a repeater, which was installed in the cable every twenty-five miles (40km) or so to boost telephone messages. The repeater, consisting of amplification devices protected by a metal casing, was heavier than the cable and had to be slowed to keep pace with it as it sank after being paid out at the stern of the cable-laying ship. The parachute canopy, of red rayon and about 14ft (4.2m) in diameter, was tugged out of its bag by the repeater as it flopped into the water. The parachute began to deploy immediately and was freed from its cargo by a hydrostatic release at a pre-determined depth. The repeater sank to its place on the ocean bed perhaps 3,500 fathoms (21,000ft; 6.4km) down. About 2,500 parachutes were put to this use by British companies in various parts of the world. The American Telephone & Telegraph

Co. employed similar methods to lay various American-designed cable systems. The idea of using parachutes in water is not a new one. Hugh Bell visualised an umbrella-like device for his aerostatic invention of 1848, as mentioned earlier.

In the 1990s there is still a big call for supply-dropping parachutes. They are extremely versatile and often immense: the biggest has touched 200ft (61m) in diameter. Depending on the size of the load, supply parachutes may be dropped in clusters, ideally three or four, for stability. Loads range from bicycles to lifeboats, vehicles, artillery and heavy oil surveying equipment. Ten tons (10,160kg) of goods on a cluster is not uncommon. The biggest single parachute load was more than 22 tons (22,350kg) of steel plate dropped from a US Hercules aircraft on six parachutes in California in 1970. Supply parachutes are made of nylon, cotton or synthetic fibre, sometimes cruciform for cheapness. In theory these are disposable, in practice usable many times over. In contrast to this simple parachute was one developed by Irvin in Canada for tactical airborne troop supply in high-level drops. The parachute canopy was reefed round its skirt to prevent opening until it had reached a low level. A radar altimeter automatically disreefed the parachute at a programmed height so that it could bring the cargo to a gentle touchdown.

In 1996 an inflatable boat, which can be parachuted into the sea for use for secret missions and has been used for the past few years by the Royal Marines, was bought by the US for its special forces. The Americans had put the Maritime Craft Air Deployment System, made by a Devon company, Aircraft Materials Ltd, under test and were so impressed that they put several on order. A rigid-hulled inflatable boat is secured to a platform, which is in turn loaded on board a Hercules C-130 aircraft. The load is then launched at altitude, a 21ft (6.4m) diameter extraction parachute pulls the load out of the plane and it freefalls until four 60ft parachutes deploy to bring it down.

Since the earliest days of man's journey beyond the bounds of the earth, the parachute has served as his insurance, unseen on the journey except to swing him back down through the atmosphere to a safe homecoming on land or water. All the manned spacecraft programmes, Russian as well as American, have depended on the parachute in their final stages, even though their methods of using it have differed slightly. When Yuri Gagarin, the world's first cosmonaut, made his first ninety-minute circuit of the earth in spaceship Vostok I in 1961, he remained in the capsule after re-entry and came down with it suspended on a parachute. Four months later another system was tried. Major Gherman Titov, in Vostok II, was flung out through an escape hatch with a rocket-powered ejection seat and came down by parachute like an escaping airman – the method adopted for subsequent Russian space missions, all of which have concluded on terra firma, not in the sea. A fault in his parachute killed one of the Russia cosmonauts in 1967. Col Vladimir Komarov, the only occupant of Soyuz (meaning 'Union') I, blasted off from Russia uneventfully early in the morning of 23 April and was soon beaming back optimistic reports on conditions and his state of health. For the next twenty-four hours all continued to go well. Then came re-entry, and disaster. His main parachute's rigging lines became entangled only forty miles (64km) above the earth. He died, a martyr to a million-to-one chance.

The United States' Mercury, Gemini and Apollo capsules all returned to splashdowns in the sea. Because of the water's cushioning effect, smaller parachutes could be used and the descent made at a higher speed than on land. Ejection seats would only have been activated had there been a mishap resulting in an off-the-launch-pad abort. Gemini's ejection seat would have shot the astronaut 900ft (274m) across the launching site and landed him on his emergency parachute in about twenty seconds. For higher altitude ejection, a 'ballute' – a self-inflated air-filled cone-shaped balloon-cum-parachute – would have helped to stabilise the astronaut after his seat had fallen away and until the main parachute filled out. For the splashdown, Mercury and Gemini capsules each came down on one parachute. Apollo was given three giant orange-and-white striped parachutes which opened out in the last stage of an automatic landing process which, viewed on the television screen, seemed as straightforward as pulling a ripcord. In fact the whole operation was a masterpiece of technological expertise and ingenious stowage.

Upon the trio of parachutes rested the entire responsibility of slowing the command module from 300mph (483kph) to a mere 22mph (35.4kph) when it hit the sea. At 23,000ft (7,000m), two white nylon conical ribbon parachutes, somewhat smaller than the RAF emergency type, blossomed out, followed by three white nylon ring-slot canopies, each about two metres in diameter. (Ring-slot canopies are made of concentric rings of fabric separated by gaps, more stable and cheaper than ribbon parachutes.) At 10,000ft (3,050m) these in turn hauled out the huge 84ft (25.6m) main

162

ring-sail parachutes. These, developed by the American company Northrop Ventura, were similar to ring-slot parachutes, but the concentric circles of fabric were fashioned into billowing vents for increased stability, which were similar in shape to the sails of a square-rigged ship. The progressive deployment of all these parachutes was triggered automatically by four barometric switches and time-delay devices, which ensured that they opened at exactly the correct height and moment.

A major mishap was narrowly avoided, however, in 1971. Television viewers watched the return of Apollo 15 uneasily as the command module of the spacecraft *Endeavour*, containing astronauts James Irwin, David Scott and Alfred Worden, plunged earthwards on only two of the three parachutes. The third dragged flaccidly above, but did not inflate. 'Be prepared for a hard impact!' they were warned. 'When I realised what had happened, it certainly gave me a strange feeling in my stomach,' Irwin told me later on a visit to London. But he realised too that there was a built-in safety margin. The system was designed to land them, if a trifle more quickly, on only two parachutes. So they and their precious 1½cwt (76kg) of moon rocks were secure. Why did the parachute fail? A major reason was that during the module's re-entry, highly inflammable fuel was jettisoned from a hot nozzle – a practice abandoned in later missions – which damaged the parachute's rigging lines.

With the end of the Apollo programme, the moon ceased to be man's principal cosmic preoccupation. Attention turned to other worlds, if not to conquer, then to explore. In October 1997 parachutes will be accompanying the Huygens probe intended to land on the surface of Titan, Saturn's biggest moon. This has a diameter of about 3,200 miles (5,150km) compared with Earth's 7,927 miles (12,756km). Christiaan Huygens, the Dutch physicist, discovered Titan in 1655, and the probe, named after him, will be carried there aboard *Cassini*, the mother-ship. If all goes well, in the year 2004 three parachutes, all of man-made fibre and designed and produced by the British company Irvin Aerospace, will transport scientific equipment through a largely nitrogen atmosphere thought to have some resemblance to that of primitive Earth, on to a surface consisting at least partially of lakes of methane. The first parachute, 8.5ft (2.5m) in diameter, will be deployed at a speed of around 870mph (1,400kph), and about 112 miles (180km) above the surface; the second, 26.5ft (8.3m) in diameter at 99 miles (160km); and the third 10ft

(3.3m) in diameter at a height of 75 miles (120km), about fifteen minutes after the first, with a total descent time of about two and a half hours.

So the parachute, the simplest of all aeronautical vehicles, will be helping man to learn more about the planets around him – an adventurous climax to its 200-year-old story. Pioneers tend to live only for the moment; it is given to few to peer round successive corners of history to chart where their ideas could lead. Other worlds, such as Saturn, were beyond the reach of anything but the telescope, and even the great Leonardo's prophetic sketches, of such as the parachute, helicopter and submarine, stopped short of a spaceship.

How distant in time and circumstance the achievement of that old parachute pioneer Garnerin seems today . . .

BIBLIOGRAPHY

Bennett, Air Vice-Marshal D. C. T., *Path Finder* (Muller, 1958).

Brickhill, Paul, *Reach for the Sky* (Collins, 1954).

Brown, W. D., *Parachutes* (Pitman, 1951).

Burbidge, William F., *From Balloon to Bomber* (John Crowther, 1946).

Caidin, Martin, *The Silken Angels* (Lippincott, 1964).

Lord Douglas of Kirtleside, and Wright, R. C., *Years of Combat* and *Years of Command* (Collins, 1963).

Dwiggins, Don, *The Story of Parachuting and Skydiving* (Collier-Macmillan, 1969).

Foot, M. R. D., *SOE in France* (HMSO, 1962).

Gatland, Kenneth, *Manned Spaceflight* (Blandford, 1971).

Gibbs-Smith, Charles H., *The Aeroplane: An Historical Survey* (HMSO, 1960).

Gibbs-Smith, Charles H., *Sir George Cayley's Aeronautics* (HMSO, 1962).

Guinness Book of Records (Guinness Publishing).

Hay, Doddy, *The Man in the Hot Seat* (Collins, 1969).

Hearn, Peter, *The Sky People* (Airlife, 1990).

Hodgson, J. E., *History of Aeronautics in Great Britain* (OUP, 1924).

Holt, L. T. C., *The Aeronauts* (Longman, 1966).

Jones, H. A., *War in the Air* (OUP, 1937).

Low, Professor A. M., *Parachutes in Peace and War* (Scientific Book Club, 1942).

Lindbergh, Charles, *We – Pilot and Plane* (GP Putnam's Sons, 1927).

Mackersey, Ian, *Into the Silk* (Robert Hale, 1956.).

Matthews, Borlase, *Aviation Pocket Book* (1916).

Neumann, G. P., *The German Air Force in the Great War* (Hodder, 1920).

Newnham, Maurice, *Prelude to Glory* (Sampson Low, 1947),

Philpott, Bryan, *Eject!, Eject!* (Ian Allan, 1989).

Saunders, H. St George, *The Red Beret* (Michael Joseph, 1949)

Sharman, Sarah, *Sir James Martin* (authorised biography). (Patrick Stephens, 1996).

Shepherd, Dolly; Peter Hearn, Molly Sedgwick, *When the 'Chute Went Up* (Robert Hale, 1984; revised edition Skyline, 1996).

Slim, Field Marshal Sir William, *Defeat Into Victory* (Cassell, 1957).

Spaight, J. M., *Air Power and War Rights* (Longman, 1947).

Tranum, John, *Nine Lives* (John Hamilton, 1933).
Wackett, Lawrence, *Aircraft Pioneer* (Angus & Robertson, 1972).
Wedgwood Benn, Capt W., *In the Sideshows* (Hodder 1919).
Wilkinson, Stephen, *Lighter Than Air* (A H Stockwell, 1930).
Willans, T. W., *Parachuting and Skydiving* (Faber, 1964).
Wingfield, R. M., *The Only Way Out* (Hutchinson, 1955).
Wright, Ian B., *Bale Out* (GMS Enterprises, 1991).

Periodicals:

Aeroplane
Annual Visitor (1803).
Chicago Daily Tribune (1919).
Daily Telegraph (1888).
Flight and Flight International
Mechanics' Magazine (1823-1872).
Morning Chronicle (1802).
Morning Herald (1802, 1837).
Morning Post (1802).
Royal Aeronautical Society Journal.
Sport Parachutist (1996).
Sports in the Sky (1996).
The Sun (1837).

INDEX